*Science of Science
and Reflexivity*

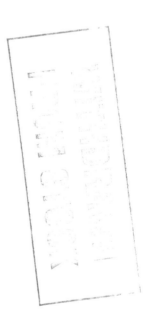

Science of Science and Reflexivity

PIERRE BOURDIEU

Translated by Richard Nice

Polity

English translation © Polity Press and The University of Chicago 2004.
First published in France as *Science de la science et réflexivité* © Éditions Raisons d'Agir, 2001.

First published in 2004 by Polity Press.

Published with the assistance of the French Ministry of Culture – National Centre for the Book.

Polity Press
65 Bridge Street
Cambridge CB2 1UR, UK

ISBN 0-7456-3059-6
ISBN 0-7456-3060-X (pbk)

A catalogue record for this book is available from the British Library.

Typeset in 10.5 on 12 pt Sabon
by Kolam Information Services Pvt. Ltd, Pondicherry, India
Printed and bound in Great Britain by TJ International, Padstow, Cornwall

For further information on Polity, visit our website: www.polity.co.uk

Contents

Foreword

Why did I choose to devote this, my final lecture course at the Collège de France, to the subject of science? And why publish it, in spite of all its limitations and imperfections? This is not a rhetorical question, and it seems to me in any case too serious to be given a rhetorical answer. I think that the world of science is threatened by a serious regression. The autonomy that science had gradually won against the religious, political or even economic powers, and, partially at least, against the state bureaucracies which ensured the minimum conditions for its independence, has been greatly weakened. The social mechanisms that were set in place as it asserted itself, such as the logic of peer competition, are in danger of being subordinated to ends imposed from outside; submission to economic interests and to the seductions of the media threatens to combine with external critiques and internal denigration, most recently presented in some 'postmodern' rantings, to undermine confidence in science and especially in social science. In short, science is in danger, and for that reason it is becoming dangerous.

There is every reason to think that the pressures of the economy are growing more intense with each day that passes, especially in areas where the products of research are highly profitable, such as medicine, biotechnology (in agriculture in particular) and, more generally, genetics – not to mention military research. Many research scientists or research teams are falling under the control of large industrial companies seeking to secure a monopoly on commercially very profitable products, through patents; and the boundary, which has long been blurred, between fundamental research, in university laboratories, and applied research, is tending to disappear completely. Disinterested scientists, who have no programme other than the one that springs from the logic of their research and who know how to make the strict minimum of concessions to 'commercial' demands to secure the funding they need for their work, risk being gradually marginalized, in some areas at least, because of the inadequacy of public support and despite the internal recognition they enjoy, in favour of vast quasi-industrial teams working to satisfy demands subordinated to the imperatives of profit. Industry and research are now so closely intertwined that not a day passes without new cases of conflict between researchers and commercial interests (for example, at the end of last year, a Californian company well known for producing a vaccine to increase defences against the AIDS virus tried to prevent publication of a scholarly paper showing that the vaccine was not effective). There is reason to fear that the logic of competition, which, as was seen in other times in the field of physics, can lead the purest of researchers to forget the economic, political or social uses that may be made of the products of their work, will combine and conjugate with more or less constrained or willing submission to the interests of firms to let whole areas of research drift little by little in the direction of heteronomy.

As for the social sciences, one might imagine that since they are not in a position to provide directly usable, that is immediately marketable, products, they would be less exposed to solicitations. In fact, however, social scientists, and especially sociologists, are the object of very great solicitude, whether it be positive – and often very profitable, materially and symbolically, for those who opt to serve the dominant vision, if only by omission (and in this case, scientific inadequacy suffices) – or negative, and malignant, sometimes even destructive, for those who, just by practising their craft, contribute to unveiling a little of the truth of the social world.

That is why it seemed to me particularly necessary to submit science to a historical and sociological analysis that in no way seeks to relativize scientific knowledge by relating and reducing it to its historical conditions, and therefore to situated and dated circumstances, but which, on the contrary, endeavours to enable those who do science to better understand the social mechanisms which orient scientific practice and so to make themselves 'masters and possessors' not only of 'nature', in accordance with the old Cartesian ambition,*

---

* 'We should make ourselves masters and possessors of nature' – Descartes, *Discours de la Méthode*, part 6 (trans.).

but also – and this is, no doubt, no less difficult – of the social world in which knowledge of nature is produced.

I wanted the printed version of this course to remain as close as possible to its oral delivery. And so, while I have removed from the transcript the repetitions and recapitulations entailed by the constraints of teaching (such as the division into lectures), and also some passages which were no doubt justified in the lecture-room context but which struck me, on rereading, as unnecessary or out of place, I have tried to render one of the most visible effects of semi-improvisation, namely the excursuses, where I stray more or less far from the main strand of the discourse: I have indicated these by transcribing them in smaller characters.

Introduction

I should like to dedicate this course to the memory of Jules Vuillemin. Little known among non-specialists, he embodied a high idea of philosophy – perhaps a little too high for our time, too high in any case to reach the audience he deserved. If I speak of him today, it is because for me he was a very great model who enabled me to continue to believe in a rigorous philosophy, at a time when I had every reason to doubt, starting with the reasons provided by the teaching of philosophy as it was then practised. He belonged to that French tradition of the philosophy of science which has been incarnated by Gaston Bachelard, Alexander Koyre and Georges Canguilhem and which is carried on today by a few others in this very institution. It is in that tradition of scientific reflection on science that what I shall try to do this year is situated.

The question I want to pose is somewhat paradoxical: can social science not help to resolve a problem that it has itself brought up, which the logicist tradition has continually confronted, and to which the 'Sokal affair' has given a new resonance – the problem posed by the historical genesis of supposedly trans-historical truths? How is it possible for a historical activity, such as scientific activity, to produce trans-historical truths, independent of history, detached from all bonds with both place and time and therefore eternally and universally valid? This is a problem that philosophers have posed more or less explicitly, especially in the nineteenth century, to a large extent under the pressure of the nascent social sciences.

To answer the question of who is the 'subject' of this 'creation of eternal verities and values' one may invoke God, or one of his substitutes, of which philosophers have invented a whole series. There is the Cartesian solution of the *semina scientiae*, the seeds or germs of science supposedly deposited in the human mind in the form of innate principles; or the Kantian solution, transcendental consciousness, the universe of the necessary conditions of knowledge which are consubstantial with thought, the transcendental subject being, in a way, the site of the a priori truths that are the principle of construction of all truth. It may be, if one follows Habermas, language, communication, etc.; or, as in early logical positivism, logical language as an a priori construction that must be imposed on reality in order for empirical science to be possible. One could also mention the Wittgensteinian solution, in which the generative principle of scientific thought is a grammar, although there is debate as to whether it is historical (with language games being subject to constraints which are historical inventions) or whether it has the form assumed by the universal laws of thought.

If we set aside theological or crypto-theological solutions – I am thinking here of the Nietzsche of *Twilight of the Idols*, who wrote: 'I fear we shall never be rid of God so long as we continue to believe in grammar' – can truth survive radical historicization? In other words, is the necessity of logical truths compatible with recognition of their historicity? Can one, then, resolve this problem without resorting to some kind of deus ex machina? Does the radical historicism which is a radical form of the death of God and all his avatars not lead one to destroy the very idea of truth, and so entail its own self-destruction? Or, on the contrary, is it possible to defend a rationalist historicism or a historicist rationalism?

To return to a more scholastic expression of this problem: are the sociology and history which relativize all knowledges by relating them to their historical conditions not condemned to relativize themselves, thus condemning themselves to a nihilistic relativism? Is it possible to escape from the forced choice between logicism and relativism, which is no doubt no more than a variant of the old controversy between dogmatism and scepticism? Logicism, which is associated with the names of Frege and Russell, is a programme for the logical foundation of mathematics which posits that there are general a priori rules for scientific evaluation and a code of immutable laws for distinguishing good from bad science. It seems to me to be an exemplary manifestation of the typically *scholastic* tendency to describe not science being done, science in the making, but science already done, a finished product from which one extracts the laws according to which it is supposedly done. The scholastic, logical or epistemological vision of science offers, as Carnap says, a 'rational reconstruction' of scientific practices, or, as Reichenbach puts it, 'a logical substitute for real processes' which is postulated as corresponding to those processes. 'Description,' said Reichenbach, 'is not a copy of real thought, but the construction of an equivalent.' Opposing the idealization of scientific practice performed by this normative epistemology, Gaston Bachelard pointed out many years ago that epistemology had thought too much about the truths of established science and not enough about the errors of science in progress, scientific activity as it actually is.

Sociologists have, to varying degrees, opened up the Pandora's box of the laboratory, and this exploration of the scientific world as it really is brings to light a whole set of facts which strongly call into question the scientific epistemology of the logicist type as I have described it and reduce scientific life to a social life with its rules, constraints, strategies, ruses, effects of domination, cheating, theft of ideas, etc. The realistic and often disenchanted vision that sociologists have thus formed of the realities of the scientific world has led them to put forward relativistic, even nihilistic, theories which are the very opposite of the official representation. There is nothing inevitable about this conclusion, and one can, in my view, combine a realistic vision of the scientific world with a realist theory of knowledge. This is on condition that one performs a twofold break with both terms of the *epistemological couple* formed by logicist dogmatism and relativism which seems inscribed in the historicist critique. We know – and Pascal pointed this out long ago – that it is the dogmatic idea or ideal of absolute knowledge that leads to scepticism: relativistic arguments have their full force only against a dogmatic and individualistic epistemology, that is to say knowledge produced by an individual scientist who confronts nature alone with his instruments (as opposed to the dialogic and argumentative knowledge of a scientific field).

One is thus led to a last question: while it is indisputable that the scientific world is a social world, one may wonder whether it is a microcosm, a field, similar (except for certain differences, which need to be specified) to all others, and in particular to the other social microcosms – the literary field, the artistic field or the legal field. Some researchers, assimilating the scientific world to the artistic world, tend to reduce laboratory activity to a semiological activity: the scientist works on 'inscriptions', he puts texts into circulation...Is it a field like others, and if it is not, what are the mechanisms that give rise to its specificity and, by the same token, make it irreducible to the history of what is generated there?

I

The state of the question

One cannot talk about such an object without exposing oneself to a permanent mirror effect: every word that can be uttered about scientific practice can be turned back on the person who utters it. This echo, this reflexivity, is not reducible to the reflexion on itself of an 'I think' (*cogito*) thinking an object (*cogitatum*) that is nothing other than itself. It is the image sent back to a knowing subject by other knowing subjects equipped with analytical tools which may have been provided to them by this knowing subject. Far from fearing this mirror – or boomerang – effect, in taking science as the object of my analysis I am deliberately aiming to expose myself, and all those who write about the social world, to a generalized reflexivity. One of my aims is to provide cognitive tools that can be turned back on the subject of the cognition, not in order to discredit scientific knowledge, but rather to check and strengthen it. Sociology, which invites the other sciences to address the question of their social foundations, cannot exempt itself from this calling into question. Casting an ironic gaze on the social world, a gaze which unveils, unmasks, brings to light what is hidden, it cannot avoid casting this gaze on itself – with the intention not of destroying sociology but rather of serving it, using the sociology of sociology in order to make a better sociology.

I will not conceal from you that I am myself somewhat daunted at having embarked on the sociological analysis of science, a particularly difficult object for several reasons. First, the sociology of science is an area that has grown enormously, at least in quantitative terms, over the last few years. This creates an initial difficulty, one of documentation, which a specialist describes very well: 'Although the social study of science is still a relatively small field, I cannot pretend to cover the entire literature. As is the case for other scholarly fields, the production of writing far outstrips anyone's ability to read a substantial portion of it. Fortunately, there is sufficient duplication, at least at a programmatic level, to enable a reader to gain a fairly confident grasp of the literature and its divisions without having to read all of it' (Lynch 1993: 83). The difficulty is compounded for someone who has not totally and exclusively devoted himself to the sociology of science. [Parenthesis: one of the major strategic choices as regards scientific investments, or, more precisely, the allocation of the finite temporal resources available to each researcher, is the choice between the intensive and the extensive – even if, as I believe, it is possible to do research that is both extensive and intensive, in particular thanks to the intensified productive efficiency that is obtained by the use of models such as that of the field, which enables one to import generic findings into each particular study, to notice specific features and to escape the ghetto effect which threatens researchers confined within a narrow specialty, such as art historians, who, as I showed last year, are often unaware of the findings of the history of education or even literary history.]

But this is not all. We are trying to understand a very complex practice (made up of problems, formulae, instruments, etc.) which can only really be mastered through a long apprenticeship. I know that some 'lab ethnographers' may turn this handicap into a privilege, convert the shortcoming into an accomplishment, and transform the outsider's situation into a deliberate 'approach', while giving themselves the air of ethnographers. On the other hand, it is not necessarily the case that the science of science is better when it is done by the 'half-pay officers' of science, defrocked scientists who have left science to go in for the sociology of science and who may have scores to settle with the science that has excluded or insufficiently recognized them: they may have the specific competence, but they do not necessarily have the posture required for the scientific implementation of that competence. In fact the solution to the problem (that of combining a very advanced technical, scientific competence – that of the cutting-edge researcher who does not have time for self-analysis – with the equally very advanced analytical competence associated with the dispositions needed to apply it in the service of a sociological analysis of scientific practice) cannot, short of a miracle, be found in and by one person alone. It no doubt lies in the construction of scientific collectives – which would presuppose that the conditions be fulfilled in order for researchers and analysts to have an interest in working together and to take the time to do it. We are clearly here in the order of utopias, since, as often in the social sciences, the obstacles to the progress of science are fundamentally social.

A further obstacle is the fact that, like the epistemologists (but less so), the most subtle analysts depend on documents (they work on archives, texts) and on what scientists say about scientific practice, and these scientists themselves depend to a large extent on the philosophy of science of the day or of an earlier period (being, like every acting agent, partially dispossessed of mastery of their own practice, they may unwittingly reproduce the sometimes inadequate or outdated epistemological or philosophical discourses with which they need to arm themselves in order to communicate their experience and to which they thereby lend their own authority).

A final and very significant difficulty is that science, and especially the legitimacy of science and the legitimate use of science, are, at every moment, at stake in struggles within the social world and even within the world of science. It follows that what is called epistemology is always in danger of being no more than a form of *justificatory discourse serving to justify science* or a particular position in the scientific field, or a spuriously neutralized reproduction of the dominant discourse of science about itself.

But I must set out explicitly why I shall start the sociology of the sociology of science that I want to outline with a social history of the sociology of science, and how I conceive such a history. Sketching this history will be a way of giving you an idea of the current state of the questions that arise in relation to science within the universe of research on science (mastery of this problematic being the real condition of entry into a scientific universe). Through it I hope to enable you to apprehend the space of positions and position-takings within which I position myself (and so give you an equivalent for that sense of the problems that characterizes the researcher engaged in the game, for whom, from the interrelationship between the various position-takings – '-isms', methods, etc. – inscribed in the field, the problematic emerges as a space of 'possibles' and as the principle of strategic choices and scientific investments). It seems to me that the space of the sociology of science is currently fairly well marked out by the three positions that I am going to examine.

In outlining such a history, one can opt either to stress the differences, the conflicts (the logic of academic institutions helps to perpetuate false alternatives), or to stress the common points, to integrate, with a practical intention of cumulation. [Reflexivity inclines

one to an integrative position which consists in bracketing-off in particular
what the opposing theories may owe to the fictitious pursuit of difference:
perhaps the best that can be derived from a history of their conflicts – of which
one has to take note – is a vision which dissolves a large part of the conflicts, in
the manner of philosophers like Wittgenstein, who have devoted much of their
careers to destroying false problems – false problems socially constituted as real
ones, especially by the philosophical tradition, and consequently very difficult
to destroy. While doing so, as a sociologist one knows that it is not sufficient to
show or even to demonstrate that a problem is a false problem in order to have
done with it.] I shall therefore take the risk of presenting a vision of the
various competing theories which will no doubt not be very 'academic', in other words not entirely in conformity with the canons of
the scholastic summary; and, out of a concern to comply with the
'principle of charity' or, rather, generosity, but also to emphasize, in
each case, what seems to me 'interesting' (from my standpoint, that is
to say, in my particular vision of science), I shall lay stress on the
theoretical or empirical *contributions* they have made – with, of
course, the ulterior motive of integrating them into my own construction. So I am very conscious of presenting them in the form of free
interpretations, or oriented reinterpretations, which at least have the
merit of presenting the *problematic* as it appears to me, the space of
possibles in relation to which I shall determine my own position.

The field of the disciplines and agents that take science as their object
– philosophy of science, epistemology, history of science, sociology of
science – a field with ill-defined frontiers, is criss-crossed by controversies and conflicts which, surprisingly, illustrate in an exemplary
way the best analyses of scientific controversies put forward by the
sociologists of science (bearing witness to the weak reflexivity of this
universe, which might have been expected to use its own gains to
monitor itself). No doubt because it is presumed to address ultimate
problems and to situate itself in the order of the 'meta', of the
reflexive, in other words at the pinnacle or foundation, it is dominated
by philosophy, whose aspirations to grandeur it borrows or mimics
(particularly through the rhetoric of the 'discourse of importance').
The sociologists and, to a lesser extent, the historians who are engaged in it remain turned towards philosophy (David Bloor fights
under the flag of Wittgenstein, even if secondarily he quotes
Durkheim; others call themselves philosophers; and the intended audience is always, visibly, that of philosophers); old philosophical problems are reactivated within it, such as that of idealism and realism (one
of the major debates around David Bloor and Barry Barnes is about

whether they are realists or idealists), or that of dogmatism and scepticism.

Another feature of this field is that relatively few empirical data are handled or demanded there, and these are generally reduced to texts, which are often drowned in interminable 'theoretical' discussions. A further characteristic of this hybrid region where all sociologists are philosophers and all philosophers are sociologists, where the (French) philosophers who concern themselves with the social sciences mingle and merge with the indeterminate devotees of the new sciences, 'cultural studies' or 'minority studies', who recklessly plunder and borrow from (French) philosophy and the social sciences, is that it is very undemanding as regards rigour in argumentation (I am thinking of the polemics around Bloor as described by Gingras (2000) and in particular the fairly systematic recourse to dishonest strategies of 'disinformation' or defamation – such as use of the label 'Marxist', a deadly but strictly political weapon, to describe someone who, like Barnes, claims allegiance with Durkheim and Mauss, or so many others; or the tendency to shift position according to the context, the interlocutor or the situation).

In recent times, the subfield of the new sociology of science (the universe mapped out by the volume edited by Pickering, *Science as Practice and Culture*, 1992) has been constituted through a series of ostentatious breaks. There has been much critique of the 'old' sociology of science. To take just one example among hundreds, Michael Lynch (1993) entitles one of his chapters: 'The demise of the "old" sociology of science'. [It is worth reflecting on such use of the opposition old / new, which is doubtless one of the obstacles to the progress of science, especially social science: sociology suffers greatly from the fact that the pursuit of distinction at any price, which prevails in certain states of the literary field, encourages an artificial emphasis on differences and prevents or delays the initial accumulation in a common paradigm – everything endlessly restarts from zero – and the establishment of strong, stable models. This is seen in particular in the use made of Kuhn's concept of the paradigm: any sociologist who feels so inclined will declare himself the bearer of a 'new paradigm', a 'new' ultimate theory of the world.] Cut off from the other specialties by a series of breaks which tend to turn it in on its own debates, traversed by countless conflicts, controversies and rivalries, this subfield is driven by the logic of supersession, of outflanking, the pursuit of an ever greater 'depth' ('deeper, more fundamental questions remain unanswered' – Woolgar 1988b: 98). Woolgar, a relativist reflexivist, endlessly refers to the inescapable, un-bypassable 'Problem' which even reflexivity cannot overcome (Collins and Yearley 1992: 307–8).

But is it legitimate to speak of a field with reference to this universe? It is certain that a number of the features I have described can be understood as field effects. For example, the fact that the irruption of the new sociology of science has had the effect, as is observed in every field, of modifying the rules of profit distribution throughout this whole universe: when it appeared that what is important and interesting is not to study scientists (the statistical relations between the properties of scientists and the success accorded to their productions), as the Mertonians do, but science, or more precisely science in progress and laboratory life, all those whose capital was linked to the old way of doing the sociology of science suffered symbolic bankruptcy and their work was relegated to the superseded past, the archaic.

It is clear that it is not easy to construct the history of the sociology of science, not only because of the vast volume of 'literature' but also because this is a field in which the history of the discipline is a stake (among others) in struggles. Each of the protagonists develops a vision of this history consistent with the interests linked to the position he occupies within the history; the different historical accounts are oriented according to the position of their producer and cannot claim the status of indisputable truth. One sees, in passing, one of the effects of reflexivity: what I have just said puts my listeners on their guard against what I am going to say, and puts me on my guard too, against the danger of privileging one orientation or against even the temptation to see myself as objective on the grounds for example that I am equally critical of all positions.

The history that I shall relate here is not inspired by the concern to aggrandize the person who delivers it by leading up by stages to the ultimate solution, capable of combining the gains in a purely additive way (in accordance with the kind of spontaneous Hegelianism that is much practised in the logic of lectures ...). It simply aims to identify and enumerate the gains – problems as much as solutions – that have to be integrated. For each of the 'moments' of the sociology of science that I distinguish (and which partially overlap), I shall try to establish on the one hand the 'cognitive style' of the current in question, and on the other hand its relationship with the historical conditions, the mood of the time.

1   An enchanted vision

The structural-functionalist tradition in the sociology of science is important in its own right, through its contributions to our knowledge of the scientific field, but also because the – now socially dominant – 'new sociology of science' has been constructed in relation to it. Although it makes many concessions to the official vision of science, this sociology does, all the same, break with the official vision of the American epistemologists: it is attentive to the contingent aspect of scientific practice (which scientists themselves may articulate in certain conditions). The Mertonians put forward a coherent description of science, which, for them, is characterized by universalism, communism or communalism (property rights are limited to the esteem or prestige linked to the fact of giving one's name to phenomena, theories, proofs, units of measurement – Heisenberg's principle, Gödel's theorem, volts, curies, roentgens, Tourette's syndrome, etc.), disinterestedness and organized scepticism. [This description is close to Weber's description of the ideal type of bureaucracy: universalism, specialized competence, impersonality and collective ownership of the function, institutionalization of meritocratic norms to regulate competition (Merton 1957a).]

Mertonian sociology of science, which (unlike the new sociology of science) is inseparable from a general theory, substitutes for a Mannheimian sociology of knowledge a sociology of researchers and scientific institutions conceived in a structural-functionalist perspective which also applies to other domains of the social world. To give a more concrete idea of the 'style' of this research, I would like to comment briefly on an article typical of Mertonian production, a quite remarkable and still valid article which needs to be integrated into the capital of gains made by the sub-discipline (Cole and Cole 1967). In the title ('Scientific output and recognition: a study in the operation of the reward system in science'), the word *recognition*, a Mertonian concept, is an express declaration of membership of a school; in their first footnote, the authors thank Merton for his 'helpful suggestions' on their work, which was financed by an institution controlled by Merton – so many social signs that this is a school united by a socially instituted cognitive style, backed by an institution. The problem addressed is a canonical one within a tradition: the next note refers to previous studies on the social factors of scientific success. Having established a correlation between quantity of publication and indices of recognition, the authors ask whether the best measure of scientific excellence is quantity or quality of output. They therefore study the relationship between the quantitative and qualitative production of 120 physicists (giving a detailed account of each moment of the methodological procedure, the sample, etc.): there is indeed a correlation, but some physicists publish many articles of little 'significance' and others a small number of articles of great 'significance'. The article enumerates the 'forms of recognition': 'honorific awards and memberships in honorific societies', medals, Nobel prizes, etc.; positions at 'top ranked departments'; citations as indices of the use made of the research by others and 'the attention the research receives from the community' (science is accepted as it presents itself). The authors test the correlations statistically (noting in passing that Nobel prize winners are much cited).

This research takes the indices of recognition, such as citation, at face value, and everything takes place as if the statistical inquiries aimed to verify that the distribution of 'rewards' is perfectly justified. This typically structural-functionalist vision is inscribed in the notion of the 'reward system' as defined by Merton: 'the institution of science has developed an elaborate system for allocating rewards to those who variously live up to its norms' (1957b: 642). 'When the institution of science works efficiently... recognition and esteem accrue to those who have best fulfilled their roles, to those who have made genuinely original contributions to the stock of knowledge' (1957b: 639). The scientific world offers a system of rewards which fulfils functions that are useful, even necessary (Merton goes on to refer to 'reinforcement by early rewards' to deserving scientists) to the functioning of the whole. [It can be seen in passing that, contrary to what some of my critics claim – I shall return to this – the replacement of 'recognition' by 'symbolic capital' is not a mere more or less gratuitous change of vocabulary, or inspired by the sheer pursuit of originality, but points to a different vision of the scientific world. Structural functionalism sees the scientific world as a 'community' which has 'developed' for itself just and legitimate regulatory institutions and where there are no struggles – or at least, no struggles over what is at stake in the struggles.]

Structural functionalism thus reveals its true nature as a collective finalism: the 'scientific community' is one of those collectives which accomplish their ends through subjectless mechanisms oriented towards ends favourable to the subjects, or at least to the best of them. 'It appears that the reward system in physics operates to give all three kinds of recognition primarily to *significant* research' (Cole and Cole 1967: 387). If the big producers publish the most important research, this is because 'the reward system operates in such a way as to encourage the creative scientists to be productive and to divert the energies of less creative scientists into other channels' (Cole and Cole 1967: 388). The reward system orients the most productive towards the most productive channels and the wisdom of the system which rewards those who deserve reward diverts the others into sidetracks such as administrative careers. [This is a secondary effect whose implications ought to be considered, especially as regards scientific productivity and equity in evaluation, and with a view to verifying whether they are really 'functional', and for whom ... One would need to consider, for example, the consequences of giving positions of authority, whether in running laboratories or in scientific administration, to second-rank researchers who, because they lack the scientific vision and the 'charismatic' dispositions needed to mobilize people's energies, often help to reinforce the forces of inertia in the scientific world.] The more that scientists are recognized (first by the educational system, then by the scientific world), the more productive they are and continue to be. The most consecrated researchers are those who were consecrated early, the 'early starters' who, thanks to their scholastic consecration, enjoy a rapid early career – appointment as assistant professor in a prestigious department for example (and 'late bloomers' are rarities). [One sees here an application of a general law of the functioning of scientific fields. Systems of selection (such as elite schools) favour great scientific careers – in two ways: first by designating those whom they select as remarkable for others and also for themselves, thus summoning them to make themselves remarked through remarkable actions, especially in the eyes of those who have remarked them (this is the concern to live up to expectations: *noblesse oblige*); on the other hand, by conferring a particular competence.]

   This approach – very objectivist, very realist (it is not questioned that the social world exists, that science exists, etc.), very classical (the most classic instruments of scientific method are brought into play) – does not make the slightest reference to the way in which scientific conflicts are settled. It accepts, in fact, the dominant – logicist – definition of science, to which it seeks to conform (even if it somewhat maltreats this paradigm). This having been said, it has the merit of bringing to light things which cannot be seen on the scale of the laboratory. This sociology of science, a central element in a whole apparatus aimed at constituting social science as a *profession*, is inspired by the intention of a 'self-vindication' of sociology on the basis of the cognitive consensus (moreover empirically verified by the school's work in the sociology of science). I am thinking in particular of the article by Cole and Zuckerman, 'The emergence of a scientific speciality: the self-exemplifying case of the sociology of science' (1975).

   [It has appeared to me retrospectively that I was somewhat unfair to Merton in my early writings in the sociology of science – no doubt under the effect of the position I then occupied, that of a newcomer in an international field dominated by Merton and structural functionalism. On the one hand I have reread the texts in a different way, on the other I have learned things about the conditions in which they were produced of which I was unaware at the time. For example, the text entitled 'The normative structure of science', which became chapter 13 of *Sociology of Science*, was first published in 1942 in a short-lived journal founded and edited by Georges Gurvitch, then a refugee in the USA: the naïvely idealistic tone of the text, which exalts democracy, science, etc., can be understood better in this context as a way of setting the scientific ideal in opposition to barbarism. I also think I was wrong to lump together with Parsons and Lazarsfeld the Merton who reintroduced Durkheim, who studied the history of science and who rejected both concept-less empiricism and data-less theoreticism, even if his attempt to escape from this choice led him into syncretism rather than a real supersession.

A remark in passing: when one is young – this is elementary sociology of science – other things being equal, one has less capital, and also less competence, and so, almost by definition, one is inclined to put oneself forward in opposition to the established figures, and therefore to look critically at their work. But this critique can in part be an effect of ignorance. In Merton's case, I was unaware not only of the context of his early writings, as I have described it, but also of his trajectory: the man I had seen – in an international conference where he was king – as an elegant, refined Wasp was in reality a recent Jewish immigrant who exaggerated an adopted 'British' elegance (in contrast to Homans, a pure product of New England, who struck me, at a dinner at Harvard, as without any mark of aristocracy – no doubt an effect of the ignorance of an outsider who is unable to recognize a certain relaxed casualness as the sign of 'real distinction'); and that disposition towards hypercorrectness, very common in first-generation immigrants undergoing integration and eager for recognition, was probably also at the root of his scientific practice and his exaltation of the 'profession' of sociology, which he wanted to establish as a scientific profession.

One sees there, it seems to me, the whole interest of the sociology of sociology: the dispositions that Merton imported into his scientific practice were at the root of his insights and his oversights – against which a true reflexive sociology could have protected him; and when one has seen this, one gains access to the ethico-epistemological principles for making (selective) use of his contributions, and more generally for subjecting authors and works of the past, and one's own relation to the authors and works of past and present, to a critical treatment that is at once epistemological and sociological.]

In an optimistic form of reflexive judgement, the scientific analysis of science as Merton practises it justifies science by justifying scientific inequalities, by showing scientifically that the distribution of prizes and rewards is in accordance with scientific justice since the scientific world proportions scientific rewards to scientists' scientific merits. It is also in order to ensure the respectability of sociology that Merton tries to make it a real scientific 'profession', modelled on the bureaucracy, and to endow the structural-functionalist spurious paradigm that he helped to construct with Parsons and Lazarsfeld with the spuriously reflexive and empirically validated crowning discipline which is the sociology of science treated as an instrument of sociodicy.

[I should like to conclude with a few observations about the scientometry which is based on the same foundations as Mertonian structural functionalism and which takes for its aim the control and evaluation of science for the purposes of 'policy-making' (the scientometric temptation hangs over the whole history of the sociology of science, as a 'crowning' science capable of awarding certificates of science; and the most modernist, and nihilist, of the new sociologists of science are not immune to this). Scientometry relies on quantitative analyses which take account only of products, in short, on compilations of scientific indicators, such as citations. The bibliometers are realists who hold that the world can be sampled, counted and measured by 'objective observers' (Hargens 1978). They provide scientific administrators with the apparently rational means of governing science and scientists and of giving scientific-looking justifications to bureaucratic decisions. One would need to examine in particular the *limits* of a method that relies on strictly quantitative criteria and which ignores the very diverse modalities and functions of citation (it can even go so far as to disregard the difference between positive and negative references). The fact remains that, despite the dubious (and sometimes deplorable) uses made of bibliometry, these methods can be used to construct sociologically useful indicators, as I did in *Homo Academicus* (1988a) to obtain an index of symbolic capital.]

2   Normal science and scientific revolutions

Although he started out as a historian of science, Thomas Kuhn radically changed the space of theoretical possibles in the sociology of science. His main contribution was to show that the development of science is not a continuous process, but is marked by a series of breaks and by the alternation of periods of 'normal science' and 'revolutions' (Kuhn 1962). Kuhn thereby introduced into the Anglo-American tradition a discontinuist philosophy of scientific development at odds with the positivist philosophy which regarded the progress of science as a continuous movement of accumulation. He also developed the idea of the 'scientific community', arguing that scientists form a closed community whose research bears on a well-defined range of problems and who use methods adapted to this work: the actions of scientists in the advanced sciences are determined by a 'paradigm', or 'disciplinary matrix', that is to say, a state of scientific achievement which is accepted by a significant proportion of scientists and which tends to be imposed on all the others.

The definition of the problems and the research methodology used flow from a professional tradition of theories, methods and competences which can only be acquired through a long training. The rules of scientific method as set out by logicians do not correspond to the reality of scientists' practices. As in other professions, scientists take for granted that the existing theories and methods are valid and they use them for their own purposes. They work not to discover new theories but to solve concrete problems, regarded as 'puzzles': for example, measuring a constant, analysing or synthesizing a compound, or explaining the functioning of a living organism. In order to do so, they use as a paradigm the traditions existing within the domain.

The paradigm is the equivalent of a language or a culture: it determines the questions that can be asked and those that are excluded, the thinkable and the unthinkable; being both 'received achievement' and a starting-point, it is a guide for future action, a programme for research to be undertaken, rather than a system of rules and norms. Consequently the scientific group is cut off from the external world so that one can analyse many scientific problems without taking account of the societies in which the scientists work. [Kuhn in fact introduces, though without developing it as such, the idea of the autonomy of the scientific universe. He thus comes to assert that this universe lies purely and simply beyond the reach of social necessity, and therefore of social science. He fails to say that in reality (and this is what the notion of the field makes it possible to understand) one of the paradoxical properties of very autonomous fields, such as science or poetry, is that they tend to have no other link with the social world than the social conditions that ensure their autonomy with respect to that world, that is to say, the very privileged conditions that are required in order to produce or appreciate very advanced mathematics or poetry, or, more precisely, the historical conditions that had to be combined to produce a social condition such that the people who benefit from them can do things of this kind.]

Kuhn's merit, as I have said, is that he has drawn attention to the discontinuities, the revolutions. But because he is content to describe the scientific world from a quasi-Durkheimian perspective, as a community dominated by a central norm, he does not seem to me to put forward a coherent model for explaining change. It is true that a particularly generous reading can construct such a model and find the motor of change in the internal conflict between orthodoxy and heresy, the defenders of the paradigm and the innovators, with the latter sometimes being reinforced, in periods of crisis, by the fact that the barriers between science and the major intellectual currents within society are then removed. I realize that through this reinterpretation I have attributed to Kuhn the essential part of my own representation of the logic of the field and its dynamic. But this is also, perhaps, a good way to show the difference between the two visions and the specific contribution of the notion of the field.

Having said this, if one sticks to the letter of what Kuhn writes, one finds a strictly *internalist* representation of change. Every paradigm reaches a point of intellectual exhaustion; the disciplinary matrix has produced all the possibles it was capable of generating (a theme that was also found, with reference to literature, in the Russian formalists), like a Hegelian essence that has realized itself, in accordance with its own logic, without external intervention. But certain 'puzzles' remain and do not find a solution.

But I should like to dwell for a moment on an argument of Kuhn's which seems to me very interesting – again, no doubt, because I reinterpret it in terms of my own model – that of 'essential tension', from the title he gave to a collection of articles (Kuhn 1977). The 'essential tension' of science is not that there is a tension between revolution and tradition, between conservatives and revolutionaries, but that revolution implies tradition, that revolutions are rooted in the paradigm: 'Revolutionary shifts of a scientific tradition are relatively rare, and extended periods of convergent research are the necessary preliminary to them. . . . Only investigations firmly rooted in the contemporary scientific tradition are likely to break that tradition and give rise to a new one' (Kuhn 1977: 227). 'The productive scientist must be a traditionalist who likes playing intricate games by pre-established rules in order to be an effective innovator who discovers new rules and new pieces with which to play them' (Kuhn 1977: 237). 'Though testing of basic commitments occurs only in extraordinary science, it is normal science that discloses both the points to test and the manner of testing' (Kuhn 1977: 272). In other words, a (true) scientific revolutionary is someone who has a great mastery of the tradition (and not someone who sweeps away the past or, more simply, just ignores it).

Thus, the 'puzzle-solving' activities of 'normal science' are based on a commonly accepted paradigm which defines, among other things, in a relatively undisputed way, what counts as a correct or incorrect solution. But in revolutionary situations the background framework which alone defines 'correctness' is itself in question. (This is exactly the problem that, in painting, Manet raised by performing a revolution so radical that it called into question the principles in whose name it could have been evaluated). This is when one is confronted with the choice between rival paradigms, and the transcendent criteria of rationality are lacking (no conciliation or compromise is possible – this is the much-discussed theme of the incommensurability of paradigms). And the emergence of a new consensus can only be explained, according to Kuhn, by non-rational factors. But from the paradox of 'essential tension' it can be concluded, reinterpreting Kuhn very freely, that the revolutionary is necessarily someone who has capital (this follows from the existence of a price of entry to the field), in other words a great mastery of the accumulated collective resources, and who therefore necessarily conserves what he supersedes.

Thus everything takes place as if, in pushing to the limit the questioning of the universal standards of rationality already prefigured in the philosophical tradition that had evolved from a Kantian-style 'transcendental' universalism to an already relativized notion of rationality – in Carnap (1950), for example, as I shall show later – Kuhn were rediscovering, with the notion of the paradigm, the Kantian tradition of the a priori, but taken in a relativized, or, more precisely, sociologized sense, as in Durkheim.

Because what appeared as the central theme of his work, namely the tension between the establishment and subversion, was in tune with the 'revolutionary' mood of the day, Kuhn, who was in no way revolutionary, was adopted, somewhat in spite of himself, as a prophet by the students of the University of Columbia and integrated into the 'counterculture' which rejected 'scientific rationality' and proclaimed the supremacy of imagination over reason. Similarly, Feyerabend was the idol of the radical students of the Freie Universität in Berlin (Toulmin 1977: 155–6, 159). The invocation of such theoretical references can be understood when one sees that the student movement took its challenge right onto the terrain of scientific life, in a university tradition where the separation between 'scholarship' and 'commitment' is particularly sharp; the aim was to liberate thought and action from the control of reason and conventions, in the social world as a whole, but also in science.

In short, this scholarly thinking owed its social force not so much to the content of the message itself – except perhaps the title, 'The structure of [...] revolutions' – as to the fact that it appeared in a historical context in which an educated population, that of students, was able to appropriate it and transform it into a *specific* revolutionary message, against academic authority. The movement of 1968 carried onto the very privileged terrain of the University a challenge that tended to call into question the deepest and most deeply undisputed principles on which the University was based, starting with the authority of science. It used scientific or epistemological weapons against the academic order which owed part of its symbolic authority to the fact that it was an *instituted episteme*, and that it was ultimately founded on an epistemology. This failed revolution shook up some essential things in the academic order, in particular the cognitive structures of those who dominated the academic and scientific order. One of the targets of the 'contestation' was orthodoxy in the social sciences and the efforts of the Capitoline triad – Parsons, Merton, and Lazarsfeld (who never got over it) – to assign itself the monopoly of the legitimate view of social science (with the sociology of science as its false closure and reflexive crown).

But the main force for resistance to the American paradigm was to appear in Europe, with, in Britain, the Edinburgh school, David Bloor and Barry Barnes, and the Bath group, with Harry Collins, and in France my article of 1975 on the scientific field (Bourdieu 1975a).

3   The 'strong programme'

David Bloor (1983) draws on Wittgenstein to ground a theory of science in which rationality, objectivity and truth are local socio-cultural norms, conventions adopted and imposed by particular groups: he takes over the Wittgensteinian concepts of 'language game' and 'form of life' which play a central role in *Philosophical Investigations*, and interprets them as referring to sociolinguistic activities associated with particular socio-cultural groups in which practices are regulated by norms conventionally adopted by the groups concerned. Scientific norms have the same limits as the groups within which they are accepted. I shall borrow from Yves Gingras a synthetic presentation of the four principles of the 'strong programme': 'In his book *Knowledge and Social Imagery*, published in 1976, with a second edition in 1991, David Bloor sets out four major methodological principles which have to be followed in order to construct a conclusive sociological theory of scientific knowledge: (1) causality: the explanation proposed must be causal; (2) impartiality: the sociologist must be impartial as regards the "truth" or "falsehood" of the assertions made by the actors; (3) symmetry: this principle states that "the same types of causes" must be used to explain both beliefs judged to be "true" by the actors and those judged to be "false"; and (4) reflexivity requires the sociology of the sciences to be subject in principle to the same treatment it applies to the other sciences. In the many case studies based on these principles, causality has been interpreted broadly enough to include the idea of understanding (thus avoiding the old dichotomy of explanation vs. understanding). Whereas the principle of impartiality is self-evident in methodological terms and has not really given rise to debate, philosophers have much debated the precise meaning and validity of the principle of symmetry. Finally, the principle of reflexivity in fact plays no part in the case studies and has only really been taken seriously by Woolgar and Ashmore, who have thus been led to study the sociology of science and its writing practices more than the sciences themselves' (Gingras 2000). I would entirely endorse this presentation and the comments it contains, only adding that in my view one cannot speak of reflexivity with respect to analyses of (other people's) sociology of the sciences which belong more to polemics than to 'the polemic of scientific reason', inasmuch as, as Bachelard suggested, this is first directed against the researcher himself.

As for Barry Barnes (1974), who makes explicit the theoretical model underlying Kuhn's analysis, he fails (like Kuhn) to raise the question of the autonomy of science, even if he refers primordially (if not exclusively) to internal factors in his search for the social causes of the belief-preferences of scientists. Social interests generate tactics of persuasion, opportunistic strategies and culturally transmitted dispositions that influence the content and development of scientific knowledge. Far from being unequivocally determined by 'the nature of things' or by 'pure logical possibilities', as Mannheim supposed, scientists' actions and the emergence and crystallization of scientific paradigms are influenced by intra- and extratheoretical social factors. Barnes and Bloor (1982) stress the *underdetermination of theory by data* (theories are never completely determined by the data they invoke, and several theories can always point to the same data); they also emphasize the fact (a commonplace for the continental epistemological tradition) that observation is oriented by theory. Controversies (made possible, once again, by underdetermination) show that the consensus is fundamentally fragile; many controversies come to an end without having been resolved by evidence alone, and stable scientific fields always contain malcontents who attribute the consensus to pure social conformism.

Harry Collins and the Bath school lay stress not so much on the relationship between interests and preferences as on the processes of interaction between scientists in and through which beliefs are formed, or, more precisely, on scientific controversies and the non-rational methods that are used to settle them. For example, Harry Collins and Trevor Pinch show that in a controversy between establishment scientists and parapsychologists both sides use strange and dishonest procedures; everything takes place as if the scientists had set up arbitrary frontiers to keep out ways of thinking and behaving that are different from their own. Collins and Pinch criticize the role of 'replication' (or conclusive experiments) in experimental science. When scientists try to reproduce other scientists' experiments, they often modify the original experimental conditions, equipment and procedures, to pursue their own programmes, whereas a perfect replication presupposes inter-changeable agents (the confrontation between Pasteur and Koch would need to be analysed in this light). Moreover, without very great familiarity with the problem in question, it is very difficult to reproduce experimental procedures from a written report. Scientific accounts aim to respect the ideal norms of scientific protocol rather than describe what really happened. Scientists may repeatedly obtain 'good' results without being able to say how they got them. When other scientists fail to 'replicate' an experiment, the original researchers may object that their procedures have not been correctly observed. In fact, the acceptance or rejection of an experiment depends on the credence given to the competence of the experimenter as much as on the strength and significance of the experimental proofs. It is not so much the intrinsic strength of the true idea that carries conviction as the social strength of the verifier. So, the scientific fact is made by the person who produces and proposes it, but also by the person who receives it (another analogy with the artistic field).

In short, like Bloor and Barnes, Collins and Pinch emphasize that experimental data are not in themselves enough to determine the extent to which an experiment counts as validating or invalidating a theory, and that it is the negotiations within a 'core set' of interested researchers that determine whether a controversy is closed. These negotiations depend to a large extent on judgements about questions of personal honesty, technical competence, institutional affiliation, style of presentation and nationality. In short, Popperian falsification-ism gives an idealized image of the solutions provided by the 'core set' of scientists in the course of their disputes.

The great virtue of Collins is that he reminds us that a fact is a collective construct and that the attested, certified fact is constructed in the interaction between the person who produces the fact and the person who receives it and tries to 'replicate' it so as to falsify or confirm it; and that he shows that processes similar to those I discovered in the world of art are also found in the scientific world. But the limits of his work result from the fact that he remains enclosed within an interactionist vision which seeks the principle of agents' actions in the interactions between them and ignores the structures (or objective relationships) and the dispositions (generally correlated with the position occupied within these structures) that are the real principle of actions and, among other things, of the interactions themselves (which may be the mediation between structures and actions). Remaining within the confines of the laboratory, he does not at all consider the *structural* conditions of the production of belief, with for example what might be called 'lab capital', brought to light by the Mertonians, who showed, for example, as we have seen, that if a discovery is made in a reputed laboratory at a prestigious university it has more chance of being validated than if it emerges in another, less well-regarded one.

4   A well-kept open secret

Laboratory studies have a clear importance inasmuch as they have broken with the rather distant and undifferentiated vision of science and moved closer to the sites of production. They thus represent an undeniable contribution, which I will sum up in the words of a member of this school, Karin Knorr-Cetina: 'Scientific objects are not only "technically" manufactured in laboratories, but are also inextricably symbolically or politically construed, for example, through literary techniques of persuasion such as one finds embodied in scientific papers, through the political stratagems of scientists in forming alliances and mobilizing resources, or through the selections and decision translations which "build" scientific findings from within' (Knorr-Cetina 1992: 115). Among the 'pioneers' of laboratory studies, I would like to mention the work of Mirko D. Grmek (1973) and Frederic L. Holmes (1974), who made use of Claude Bernard's laboratory notebooks to analyse various aspects of his work. One sees there how even the best scientists dismiss unfavourable results as aberrations which they exclude from their official accounts, how they sometimes transform equivocal experiments into decisive results, or modify the order in which experiments were conducted, etc., and how they all comply with the common rhetorical strategies that are required in the shift from private laboratory notes to publications.

But here I must quote Medawar, who sums up very well the distortions that result from relying purely on published accounts: 'findings appear more decisive and more honest; the most creative aspects of the research disappear, giving the impression that imagination, passion, art have played no part in them and that the innovation results not from the passionate activity of deeply committed hands and brains but from passive submission to the sterile precepts of the so-called "Scientific Method". This impoverishment leads to the ratification of an old-fashioned and naïve empiricist or inductivist view of research practice' (Medawar 1964).

On the basis of a study of a laboratory in which she minutely studied the successive drafts of a document which led to a publication after passing through sixteen different versions, Karin Knorr-Cetina analyses in detail the transformations of the rhetoric of the text, the work of depersonalization carried out by the authors, etc. (One's only regret is that, rather than going in for long theoretico-philosophical debates with Habermas, Luhmann, etc., she does not give the strictly sociological information about the authors and their laboratory that would enable one to relate the rhetorical strategies to the position of the laboratory in the scientific field and the dispositions of the agents engaged in the production and circulation of the drafts.)

However, the most accurate and complete account of the achievements of this tradition that I have found is that by G. Nigel Gilbert and Michael Mulkay (1984). They show that scientists' discourse varies according to the context, and they distinguish two 'repertoires' (it seems to me it would be better to say two rhetorics). The 'empiricist repertoire' is characteristic of formal experimental research papers which are written in accordance with the empiricist representation of scientific action: the style must be impersonal and minimize reference to social actors and their beliefs so as to produce all the appearances of objectivity; references to the dependence of the observations on theoretical speculations disappear; everything is done to mark the scientist's distance from his model; the account given in the 'methods' section is expressed in the form of general formulae. Then there is the 'contingent repertoire', which coexists with the first: when scientists speak informally, they stress their dependence on an 'intuitive feel for research', which is inevitable given the practical character of the operations in question (Gilbert and Mulkay 1984: 53). These operations cannot be written out and they can only really be understood through close personal contact. The authors speak of 'practical skills', traditional knacks, 'recipes' (researchers often make comparisons with cooking). Research is a customary practice, learned by example. Communication is set up between people who share the same 'background' of problems and technical assumptions. It is remarkable that, as the authors point out, scientists spontaneously return to the language of the 'contingent repertoire' when they talk about what other people do or offer their sceptical reading of other people's official protocols.

In short, scientists use two linguistic registers: in the 'empiricist repertoire', they write in a conventionally impersonal manner; by minimizing the references to human intervention, they construct texts in which the physical world seems literally to act and speak for itself. When the author is authorized to appear in the text, he is presented either as forced to undertake the experiments, or to reach the theoretical conclusions, by the unequivocal demands of the natural phenomena he is studying, or as rigidly constrained by rules of experimental procedure. In less formal situations, this repertoire is complemented and sometimes contradicted by a repertoire which stresses the role played by personal contingencies in action and belief. The asymmetrical account which presents the correct belief as springing indisputably from the experimental proof and the incorrect belief from the effect of personal, social and generally non-scientific factors, reappears in studies of science (which most often largely rely on formal accounts).

What sociology brings to light is in fact known and even belongs to the realm of 'common knowledge', as economists call it. Private discourse on the private aspect of research seems almost designed to recall to modesty the sociologist who might be tempted to think that he is discovering the 'inner workings' of science, and should in any case be treated with much reflexion and delicacy. It would take great quantities of refined phenomenology to analyse these phenomena of dual consciousness associating and combining – like all forms of *bad faith* (in the Sartrian sense) or self-deception – knowledge and the refusal to know, knowledge and refusal to know that one knows, knowledge and refusal to let other people say what one knows, or worse, *that* one knows. (One would have to say the same of career 'strategies' and, for example, choices of specialty or object of study, which cannot be described in terms of the ordinary alternatives of awareness and unawareness, calculation and innocence.) All these games of individual bad faith are only possible in a profound complicity with a group of scientists.

But I should like to mention in more detail the last chapter, entitled 'Joking apart'. The authors point out that when they go into laboratories, they find, often pinned to the walls, curious texts such as a 'Dictionary of useful research phrases', which circulate from lab to lab, and give examples of the ironic and parodic discourse about scientific discourse which scientists themselves produce: 'Postprandial Proceedings of the Cavendish Physical Society', 'Journal of Jocular Physics', 'Journal of Irreproducible Results', 'Review of Unclear Physics'.

Along the lines of the 'do say...don't say ...' lists found in language manuals, the authors draw up a comparative table contrasting two versions of what goes on, the one that is produced for formal presentation, and the informal account of what really happened. On the one hand, 'What he wrote', on the other, 'What he meant' (Gilbert and Mulkay 1984: 176):

What he wrote	*What he meant*
(a) It has long been known that...	I haven't bothered to look up the reference.
(b) While it has not been possible to provide definite answers to these questions...	The experiment didn't work out, but I figured I could at least get a publication out of it.
(c) The W-PO system was chosen as especially suitable...	The fellow in the next lab had some already prepared.
(d) Three of the samples were chosen for detailed study...	The results on the others didn't make sense and were ignored.
(e) Accidentally strained during mounting...	Dropped on the floor.
(f) Handled with extreme care throughout the experiment ...	Not dropped on the floor.
(g) Typical results are shown...	The best results are shown, i.e. those that fit the dogma.
(h) Agreement with the predicted curve is:	
Excellent	Fair
Good	Poor
Satisfactory	Doubtful
Fair	Imaginary
(i) Correct within an order of magnitude...	Wrong.
(j) Of great theoretical and practical importance...	Interesting to me.
(k) It is suggested that...it is believed that...it appears that...	I think.
(l) It is generally believed that...	A couple of other guys think so too.
(m) The most reliable results are those obtained by Jones...	He was my graduate student.
(n) Fascinating work...	Work by a member of our group.
(o) Of doubtful significance...	Work by someone else.

This table produces a humorous effect by exposing the hypocrisy of the formal literature. But the dual truth of the experience that agents may have of their own practice has something universal about it. One knows the truth of what one does (for example, the more or less arbitrary or in any case contingent character of the reasons or causes which determine a judicial decision), but to keep in line with the official idea of what one does, or with the idea one has of oneself, this decision must appear to have been motivated by reasons, and by reasons that are as elevated (and juridical) as possible. Formal discourse is hypocritical, but the propensity to 'radical chic' leads people to forget that the two truths coexist, with more or less difficulty, in the agents themselves (this is a truth that I took a long time to learn and that I learned, paradoxically, from the Kabyles, perhaps because it is easier to understand other people's collective hypocrisies than one's own). Among the forces that support social rules there is the imperative of *regularization*, manifest in the fact of 'falling into line with the rule', which leads people to present practices which may be in complete transgression of the rule as being performed in accordance with the rule, because the essential thing is to save the rule (and this is why the group approves and respects this collective hypocrisy). It is a matter of saving the particular interests of a particular scientist who broke his pipette; but also, and at the same time, of saving the collective belief in science which means that, although everyone knows that things do not happen the way people say they happen, everyone carries on as if they happened that way. And this raises the very general problem of the function or effect of sociology, which, in many cases, makes public the 'denied' things that groups know and 'do not want to know'.

One would therefore be tempted to ratify the – it seems to me, fairly indisputable – conclusion reached by Gilbert and Mulkay, or Peter Medawar, if it were not most often associated with a philosophy of action (and a cynical vision of practice) which is fully developed in most of the writings devoted to 'laboratory life'. For example, while it is no doubt true that, as Karin Knorr-Cetina says, the laboratory is a place where actions are performed with a view to 'making things work' (she quotes Lynch: 'The vernacular formulation of "making it work" suggests a contingency of results upon "skilled production"...Making it work entails a selection of those "effects" that can be traced to "rational" sets of contingencies and a discarding of "attempts" that are bound to fall short of such "effects"' (Lynch 1982: 161, quoted by Knorr-Cetina 1983: 120)), it is impossible to accept the idea she expresses in the sentence I cited earlier, where she slides from the assertion, which is at the centre of my first article, of the *inseparably scientific and social* character of researchers' strategies, to the assertion of a symbolic *and political* construction based on 'techniques of persuasion' and 'stratagems' aimed at building alliances. The simultaneously scientific and social 'strategies' of the scientific habitus are envisaged and treated as *conscious*, not to say *cynical*, *stratagems*, oriented towards the glory of the researcher.

But I must now turn, to conclude, to a branch of the socio-philosophy of science that has developed mainly in France, but which has enjoyed some success on the campuses of English-speaking universities: I mean the works of Latour and Woolgar and, in particular, *Laboratory Life*, which gives an enlarged image of all the aberrations of the new sociology of science (Latour and Woolgar 1979). This current is very strongly marked by the historical conditions, so that I fear I shall find it difficult to distinguish, as I have for the previous currents, the analysis of the theses in question from the analysis of their social conditions of production. [For example, in a would-be benevolent 'summary' of *Laboratory Life*, one reads: 'The laboratory deals with inscriptions (in Derrida's terms), utterances (in Foucault's terms); constructions which make the realities they evoke. These constructions are imposed through the negotiation of the small groups of researchers concerned. Verification (assay) is self-verification; it creates its own truth; it is self-verifying because there is nothing to verify it with. *Laboratory Life* describes the process of verification as a process of negotiation'.]

It is posited that the products of science are the result of a process of manufacture and that the laboratory, itself an artificial universe, cut off from the world in countless ways, physically, socially and also by the capital of instruments that is handled there, is the site of the construction, even the 'creation', of the phenomena with which we build up and test theories and which would not exist without the instrumental equipment of the laboratory. 'The artificial reality that the participants describe as an objective entity, has in fact been constructed.'

Starting from this observation, which for anyone familiar with Bachelard is hardly stunning, it is possible, by playing on words or letting words play, to move to apparently radical propositions (calculated to make big waves, especially on American campuses dominated by the logical-positivist vision). By saying that facts are artificial in the sense of manufactured, Latour and Woolgar intimate that they are fictitious, not objective, not authentic. The success of this argument results from the 'radicality effect', as Yves Gingras (2000) has put it, generated by the slippage suggested and encouraged by a skilful use of ambiguous concepts. The strategy of *moving to the limit* is one of the privileged devices in the pursuit of this effect (I remember the use made in the 1970s of Illich's thesis of 'deschooling society' to counter the description of the reproductive effect of the educational system); but it can lead to positions that are untenable, unsustainable, because they are simply absurd. From this comes a typical strategy, that of advancing a very radical position (of the type: the scientific fact is a construction or – *slippage* – a fabrication, and therefore an artefact, a fiction) before beating a retreat, in the face of criticism, back to banalities, that is, to the more ordinary face of ambiguous notions like 'construction', etc.

But to produce this effect of 'derealization', the authors do not simply stress the contrast between the improvised character of real laboratory practices and experimental reasoning as rationally reconstructed in textbooks and research reports. Latour and Woolgar highlight the very important role of *texts* in the *fabrication of facts as fiction*.

They argue that the researchers they observed during their ethnography at the Salk Institute did not investigate things in themselves; rather, they dealt with 'literary inscriptions' produced by technicians working with recording instruments: 'Between scientists and chaos there is nothing but a wall of archives, labels, protocol books, figures, and papers ...' 'Despite the fact that our scientists held the belief that the inscriptions could be representations or indicators of some entity with an independent existence "out there", we have argued that such entities were constituted solely through the use of these inscriptions' (Latour and Woolgar 1979: 245, 128). In short, the researchers' naïvely realist belief in a reality external to the laboratory is a pure illusion, from which only a realist sociology can rid them.

Once the final product has been worked out in circulation, the intermediate stages that made it possible, in particular the vast network of negotiations and machinations that have given rise to the acceptance of a fact, are forgotten, not least because researchers wipe away the traces of their research as they move on. Because scientific facts are constructed, communicated and evaluated in the form of written statements, scientific work is largely a literary and interpretative activity: 'A fact is nothing but a statement with no modality – M – and no trace of authorship' (Latour and Woolgar 1979: 82); the work of circulation will lead to the removal of the modalities, in other words the indicators of temporal or local reference (for example, 'these data *may* indicate that ...', 'I *believe* this experiment shows that ...'), in short, all 'indexical' expressions. The researcher must reconstruct the process of consecration and universalization through which the fact gradually comes to be recognized as such – publications, networks of citations, disputes between rival laboratories and negotiations among members of a research group (which means, for example, the social conditions in which the hormonal factor, TRF, was stripped of contentious qualifications); he must describe how a judgement was transformed into a fact and so freed from the conditions of its production (now forgotten both by the producer and the receivers).

Latour and Woolgar seek to adopt the point of view of an observer who sees what happens in the laboratory without sharing the researchers' beliefs. Making a virtue of necessity, they describe what seems to them intelligible in the laboratory: the traces, the texts, the conversations, the rituals, and the strange material (one of the high points of this work is the 'stranger's' description of a simple instrument, a pipette... – Woolgar 1988b: 85). They can thus treat natural science as a literary activity, and, to describe and interpret this circulation of scientific products, they draw on a semiological model (that of A. J. Greimas). They attribute the privileged status of the natural sciences not to the particular validity of their discoveries but to the expensive equipment and institutional strategies which transform natural elements into practically impregnable texts, with the author, the theory, nature and the public being so many 'text effects'.

The *semiological vision of the world* which induces them to emphasize the traces and signs leads them to that paradigmatic form of the scholastic bias, *textism*, which constitutes social reality as text (in the manner of some ethnologists, like Marcus (Marcus and Fischer 1986) or even Geertz, or some historians, who, with the 'linguistic turn' at about the same time, started to say that everything is text). Science is then just a discourse or a fiction among others, but one capable of exerting a 'truth effect' produced, like all other literary effects, through textual characteristics such as the tense of verbs, the structure of utterances, modalities, etc. (The absence of any attempt at prosopography condemns them to seek the power of texts in the texts themselves.) The universe of science is a world which succeeds in imposing universally the belief in its fictions.

The semiological prejudice is most clearly seen in *The Pasteurization of France* (Latour 1988), in which Latour treats Pasteur as a textual signifier inserted in a story which weaves together a heterogeneous network of agencies and entities, daily life on the farm, sexual practices and personal hygiene, architecture and the therapeutic regime of the clinic, sanitary conditions in towns and the microscopic entities encountered in the laboratory, in short a whole world of representations that Pasteur constructs and through which he presents himself as the eminent scientist. [I would like, as it were *a contrario*, to mention here a work which, being based on a meticulous reading of a good part of Pasteur's 'laboratory notebooks', gives a realistic and well-informed view, but without ostentatious display of gratuitous theoretical effects, of Pasteur's undertaking, but also (chapter 10) of the Pasteur 'myth': G. L. Geison, *The Private Science of Louis Pasteur* (1995).]

Semiologism combines with a naïvely Machiavellian view of scientists' strategies: the symbolic actions they perform to win recognition for their 'fictions' are at the same time influence-seeking and power-seeking strategies through which they pursue their own glorification. So the question is how a man named Pasteur built alliances and proselytized to impose a research programme. With all the ambiguity that results from treating semiological entities as socio-historical descriptors, Latour treats Pasteur as a kind of semiological entity who acts historically, and who acts as any capitalist would act (one can read in this light the interview entitled 'The last of the wild capitalists' (Latour 1983), in which Latour endeavours to show that the scientist aware of his symbolic interests is the most accomplished form of the capitalist entrepreneur, all of whose actions are guided by the pursuit of maximized profit). Rather than seeking the principle of actions where it really lies, in positions and dispositions, Latour can only try to find it in conscious (even cynical) influence and power strategies (thus regressing from a Mertonian collective finalism to a finalism of individual agents) – and the science of science is reduced to the description of alliances and struggles for symbolic 'credit'.

Having been accused by the advocates of the 'strong programme' of practising disinformation and using scientifically dishonest strategies, Latour, who, in all the rest of his work appears as a radical constructivist, has recently made himself the champion of realism, invoking the social role he gives to objects, and in particular manufactured objects, in his analysis of the scientific world. He proposes to do nothing less than challenge the distinction between human agents (or forces) and non-human agents. But the most astonishing example is that of the door and the automatic door closer, called in French a 'groom' by analogy with the human groom or butler, which Latour invokes in an article entitled 'Where are the missing masses?' (1993), with a view to finding in things the constraints that are missing (the 'missing masses', a chic scientific reference) in the ordinary analysis of the political and social order. Although they are mechanical objects, doors and technical devices act as constant constraints on our behaviour and the effects of the intervention of these 'actants' are indistinguishable from those exerted by a moral or normative control: a door lets us pass through a certain point in the wall and at a certain speed; a mechanical policeman controls the traffic like a real policeman, the computer on my desk requires me to write it instructions in a particular syntactic form. The 'missing masses' (analogous to those that explain the value of the rate of expansion of the universe, no less ...) lie in the technical objects that surround us. We delegate to them the status of actors and also power. To understand these technical objects and their power, do we need to study the technical science of their operation? (This is no doubt easier with a door or a pipette than with a cyclotron

...) If not, then what method must we use to discover the fact of 'delegation' and what is delegated to these remarkable 'actants'? We simply have to resort to the method, well known to economists, of 'counterfactual hypotheses', and thus, in seeking to understand the power of doors, to imagine what life would be like if they did not exist. You draw up a double-entry table: on one side, what you would have to do if there were no door; on the other, the slight effort of pulling or pushing which achieves the same result. So a big effort is turned into a smaller, and the operation thus brought to light by the analyst is what Latour proposes to call 'displacement or translation or delegation or shifting': 'we have delegated to the hinge the work of reversibly solving the hole-wall dilemma.' And to conclude, one arrives at a general law: 'every time you want to know what a non-human does, simply imagine what other humans or other non-humans would have to do were this character not present. This imaginary substitution exactly sizes up the role, or function, of this little figure.' All power to the (scientific) imagination. The trivial difference between human and non-human agents has disappeared (the 'groom' takes the place of a person and shapes human action by prescribing who can go through the door) and one can freely dissertate upon the way we delegate power to technical objects... To show that what might be seen as a mere literary game is in fact the expression of the 'methodological' approach of a 'school', I could also have mentioned Michel Callon (1986), who, in his study of scallops, places on the same footing fishermen, scallops, seagulls and the wind, as elements in a 'system of actants'. But I will leave it at that...

[I cannot help feeling some unease at what I have just done. On the one hand, I would not want to give this work the importance it gives itself and even risk helping to give it value by pushing the critical analysis beyond what this kind of text deserves, though I think it a good thing that there are people willing to devote time and energy to ridding science of the dire effects of philosophical hubris as Jacques Bouveresse (1999) has done for Régis Debray, or Yves Gingras (1995) for the same Latour. But, on the other hand, I have in mind a very fine article by Jane Tompkins (1988), who describes the logic of 'righteous wrath', the 'sentiment of supreme righteousness' of the hero of a Western who, having been 'unduly victimized', may be led to 'do to the villains things which a short while ago only the villains did': in the academic or scientific world, this sentiment can lead someone who feels invested with the mission of doing justice to commit a 'bloodless violence' which, while remaining within the limits of academic propriety, is inspired by a rage no less strong than that which led the hero to do justice himself. And Jane Tompkins points out that this legitimate fury may lead one to feel justified in attacking not only the faults and failings of a text but the most personal properties of the person. Nor will I conceal the fact that behind the 'discourse of importance' (an essential part of which is devoted to asserting the importance of the discourse – I'm referring to the analysis I made of the rhetoric of Althusser and Balibar (Bourdieu 2001b)), its incantatory and self-legitimating formulae (one is 'radical', 'counterintuitive', 'new'), its peremptory tone (designed to overwhelm), I was pointing to the dispositions statistically associated with a particular social origin (it is certain that dispositions towards arrogance, bluff, even imposture, the quest for the effect of radicality, etc., are not equally distributed among researchers depending on their social origin, their sex, or more precisely their sex *and* their social origin). And I could not refrain from suggesting that if this rhetoric has enjoyed a social success disproportionate to its merits, this is perhaps because the sociology of science occupies a very special position within sociology, on the ill-defined border between sociology and philosophy, so that it is possible there to avoid a real break with philosophy and with all the social profits associated with being able to call oneself a philosopher in certain markets; such a break is long and costly, presupposing the hardwon acquisition of technical instruments and many unrewarding investments in activities regarded as inferior, even unworthy. Socially constituted dispositions towards audacity and facile radicalism which, in scientific fields more capable of imposing their controls and censorship, would have had to be tempered and sublimated, have found there a terrain on which they can express themselves without any mask or constraint. Having said that, my 'righteous anger' has in my view a justification in the fact that these people, who often refuse the name and the contract of sociologists without really being able to submit to the constraints of philosophical rigour, may enjoy some success among new entrants and hold back the progress of research by disseminating false problems which waste much time, overall, by leading some into cul-de-sacs and others, who have better things to do, into an effort of critique, often somewhat desperately, such is the power of the social mechanisms capable of sustaining error. I am thinking in particular of the *allodoxia*, the erroneous conception of the identity of persons and ideas, which prevails particularly with respect to all those who occupy the uncertain regions between philosophy and the social sciences (and also journalism), and who, situated either side of the frontier – just outside, like Régis Debray, with his scientific metaphors mimicking the external signs of scientificity (Gödel's theorem, which provoked Jacques Bouveresse's 'righteous anger') and his pseudo-scientific label, 'mediology', or just inside, like our sociologist-philosophers of science – are particularly able and particularly well placed to inspire a misplaced credence, *allodoxia*, by playing on all the double games, guaranteeing all the double profits secured by the combination of several registers of authority and importance, including that of philosophy and that of science.]

II

A world apart

One of the central points on which I part company with all the analyses I have discussed is the concept of the field, which emphasizes the *structures* which orient scientific practices and whose efficacy is exerted at the micro-sociological level, where most of the works I have criticized, in particular laboratory studies, are located. To give an idea of the limits of these studies one could see them as equivalent, in a quite different domain, to old-style village monographs (and even a substantial proportion of ethnographic studies), which took as their object social micro-units that were presumed to be autonomous (if indeed that question was addressed at all) – isolated, delimited universes that were thought to be easier to study because the data presented themselves, as it were, already prepared on that scale (with census records, local land registers, etc.). The laboratory, a small, closed and separate universe, presenting protocols all ready for analysis, laboratory journals, archives, etc., similarly seems to invite a monographic, idiographic approach.

But it is immediately clear that a laboratory is a social microcosm, itself situated in a space containing other laboratories, these together constituting a discipline (itself situated in a hierarchized space, that of the disciplines), and that it derives a major part of its properties from the position it occupies within that space. If one ignores this series of structural interlockings, this (relational) position and the associated effects of position, one is likely, as in the case of the village monograph, to look in the laboratory for explanatory principles which in fact lie outside it, in the structure of the space within which it is located. Only through an overall theory of the scientific space, which understands it as a space structured according to both generic and specific logics, is it possible truly to understand a given point in this space, whether a particular laboratory or an individual researcher.

The notion of the field marks a first break with the interactionist approach, inasmuch as it takes note of the existence of this structure of objective relationships among laboratories and among researchers which governs or orients practices. It makes a second break, inasmuch as the relational or structural approach that it introduces is associated with a dispositionalist philosophy, which breaks with the finalism, allied to a naïve intentionalism, which sees agents – in this case researchers – as rational calculators seeking not so much the truth as the social profits accruing to those who appear to have discovered it.

In an article published a good many years ago now (1975a), I put forward the idea that the scientific field, like other fields, is a structured field of forces, and also a field of struggles to conserve or transform this field of forces. The first part of the definition (a field of forces) corresponds to the physicalist stage of sociology conceived as a social physics. The agents, isolated scientists, teams or laboratories, create, through their relationships, the very space that determines them, although it only exists through the agents placed in it, who, to use the language of physics, 'distort the space in their neighbourhood', conferring a certain structure upon it. It is in the relationship between the various agents (conceived as 'field sources') that the field and the relations of force that characterize it are generated (a specific, symbolic relation of force, given the 'nature' of the force capable of being exerted in this field – scientific capital, a form of symbolic capital which acts in and through communication). More precisely, it is the agents, that is to say the isolated scientists, teams or laboratories, defined by the volume and structure of the specific capital they possess, that determine the structure of the field that determines them, in other words the state of the forces that are exerted on scientific production, on the scientists' practices. The weight associated with an agent, who undergoes the forces of the field at the same time as he helps to structure it, depends on all the other agents, all the other points in the space, and the relations among those points, that is to say, the whole space (those familiar with the principles of multiple correspondence analysis will appreciate the affinity between that method of mathematical analysis and thinking in terms of a field).

The force attached to an agent depends on his various 'assets', differential factors of success which may give him an advantage in the competition, that is to say, more precisely, the volume and structure of the capital in its various forms that he possesses. Scientific capital is a particular kind of symbolic capital, a capital based on knowledge and recognition. It is a power which functions as a form of credit, presupposing the trust or belief of those who undergo it because they are disposed (by their training and by the very fact of their belonging to the field) to give credit, belief. The structure of the distribution of capital determines the structure of the field, in other words the relations of force among the scientific agents: possession of a large quantity (and therefore a large share) of capital gives a power over the field, and therefore over agents (relatively) less endowed with capital (and over the price of entry to the field) and governs the distribution of the chances of profit.

Even in the absence of any direct interaction, intervention or manipulation, the structure of the field, defined by the unequal distribution of capital, that is of the specific weapons or assets, bears on all the agents within it, restricting more or less the space of possibles that is open to them, depending on how well placed they are within the field, that is within this distribution. A dominant agent is one who occupies a place within the structure such that the structure works in his favour. [These very general principles – which are also valid in other fields, the economy, for example – make it possible to understand the phenomena of communication and circulation of which the scientific field is the site, and which a purely 'semiological' interpretation cannot fully explain. One of the virtues of the notion of the field is that it not only provides general principles for understanding social universes which take the form of a field, but also obliges one to ask questions about the specificity that these general principles take on in each particular case. The questions that I shall ask about the scientific field will be of two types: on the one hand, whether one finds there the general properties of fields; and on the other hand whether this particular universe has a specific logic, linked to its specific ends and to the specific characteristics of the games that are played there. The theory of the field orients and governs empirical research. It forces the researcher to ask what people are 'playing at' in this field (purely on the basis of experience, and so with the risk, most of the time, of falling into a positive form of the hermeneutic circle), what are the stakes, the goods or properties sought and distributed or redistributed, and how they are distributed, what are the instruments or weapons that one needs to have in order to play with some chance of winning, and what is, at each moment in the game, the structure of the distribution of goods, gains and assets, that is of the specific capital (the notion of the field, it can be seen, is a system of questions that are specified each time).]

We can now move to the second stage of the definition – the field as a field of struggles, a socially constructed field of action in which agents endowed with different resources confront one another to conserve or transform the existing power relations. Agents undertake actions there, the ends, means and efficacy of which depend on their position within the field of forces, their position within the structure of the distribution of capital. Each scientific act, like every practice, is the product of the encounter between two histories, a history embodied, incorporated in the form of dispositions, and a history objectified in the very structure of the field and in technical objects (instruments), writings, etc. The specificity of the scientific field is partly due to the fact that the quantity of accumulated history is especially great, owing in particular to the 'conservation' of its achievements in a particularly economical form, with for example organization into principles and formulae or in the form of a slowly accumulated stock of calibrated actions and routinized skills. Rather than being deployed in the context of a universe without gravity or inertia, where they would be able to develop without restriction, researchers' strategies are oriented by the objective constraints and possibilities implied in their respective position and by the representation (itself linked to their position) they are able to form of their position and those of their rivals, on the basis of their information and their cognitive structures.

The room for manoeuvre available to their strategies will depend on the structure of the field, characterized for example by a more or less high degree of concentration of capital (ranging from near-monopoly – an example of which I analysed last year with regard to the Académie des Beaux-Arts in the time of Manet – to a virtually equal distribution among all competitors); but it will always be organized around the principal opposition between the dominant (those whom economists sometimes call 'first movers', highlighting the capacity for initiative that they enjoy) and the dominated, the challengers. The former are able, often effortlessly, to impose the representation of science most favourable to their interests, that is to say, the 'correct', legitimate way to play and the rules of the game and therefore of participation in the game. Their interests are bound up with the established state of the field and they are the natural defenders of the 'normal science' of the day. They enjoy decisive advantages in the competition, one reason being that they constitute an obligatory reference point for their competitors, who, whatever they do, are willy-nilly required actively or passively to take up a position in relation to them. The threats that the challengers present to them force them to maintain constant vigilance and they can only maintain their position through permanent innovation.

Strategies and their chances of success depend on the position occupied within the structure. That being so, it may be wondered how real transformations of the field can occur, given that the forces of the field tend to reinforce the dominant positions – bearing in mind, however, that, as in the domain of the economy, changes within a field are often determined by redefinitions of the frontiers between fields, linked (as cause or effect) to the sudden arrival of new entrants endowed with new resources. This explains why the boundaries of the field are almost always at stake in the struggles within the field. (I shall later give some examples of scientific 'revolutions' linked to the move from one discipline to another.)

I do not want to conclude this reminder of theoretical schemata without saying that the laboratory itself is a field (a subfield) which, while defined by a determinate position within the field of the discipline as a whole, has a relative autonomy with respect to the constraints associated with that position. As a specific 'space of play', it helps to determine the strategies of the agents, that is to say, the possibilities and impossibilities offered to their dispositions. Research strategies depend on the position occupied in the subfield of the laboratory, which means, once again, the position of each researcher within the structure of the distribution of capital in its two kinds, strictly scientific and administrative. Terry Shinn (1988) provides a remarkable demonstration of this in his analysis of the division of labour in a physics laboratory, and it also emerges from Heilbron and Seidel's description (1989) of the Berkeley physics laboratory, with the opposition between Oppenheimer and Lawrence.

Laboratory studies have tended to forget the effect of the laboratory's position within a structure; but there is also an effect of position in the structure of the laboratory, a typical example of which is found in Heilbron and Seidel's book (1989), with the story of a certain Jean Thibaud: this young physicist in Louis de Broglie's laboratory invented the cyclotron method which made proton acceleration possible with a small machine, but he did not have sufficient means to develop his project and above all 'he did not have someone like Lawrence to support him', that is to say, the institutional structure and the institutional leadership of a man such as Lawrence, a bidimensional figure, possessing both scientific and administrative authority, capable of creating belief, conviction, and of securing the social support for belief, for example by obtaining posts for young researchers.

This brief reminder seemed necessary, not least because my article has been the object of many borrowings, whether overt or disguised – one of the most skilful ways of concealing these being to accompany them with the critique of an imaginary text against which one can sometimes argue exactly what the criticized text put forward. I will give only one example, that of Karin Knorr-Cetina, one of the first to draw on my article, which she initially cited very positively, then more and more distantly, up to the point of the critique that I shall analyse, where there remains almost nothing of what I wrote, or what she initially seemed to have understood from it. She complains that the model I put forward is 'dangerously near to that of classical economic theory' and (making herself more Catholic than the Pope!) that it contains no theory of exploitation, since it fails to 'distinguish between scientists-capitalists and scientists-workers'; that I make the agent 'a conscious maximizer of profits', since I 'ignore the fact that outcomes are often not *consciously* calculated' (in an earlier text, she said exactly the contrary and invoked the habitus). Finally, she believes that no more than 'a substitution of terms' is involved in referring to symbolic capital rather than 'recognition' (Knorr-Cetina 1983: 130–1). [This critique appears in a collection of texts, a typical product of an academic-publishing operation aiming to give visibility to a set of authors with similar theoretical positions. These 'non-books', as the Americans so accurately describe them, a category which should also include manuals, have a salient social function: they canonize (another name for them is 'selected extracts') and they categorize, distinguishing subjectivists and objectivists, individualists and holists – structuring distinctions which generate (false) problems. One would need to analyse the whole set of instruments of knowledge, of concentration and accumulation of knowledge, which, because they are also instruments of accumulation and concentration of academic capital, orient knowledge on the basis of considerations (or strategies) of academic power, control of science, etc. For example, dictionaries – of sociology, ethnology, philosophy, etc. – are often bids for power, inasmuch as they make it possible to legislate while appearing to describe. Functioning as instruments of construction of the reality that they pretend to record, they can give existence to authors or concepts that do not exist, ignore concepts or authors that do exist, etc. People often forget that a very significant part of the sources used by historians is the product of such construction work.]

If I have discussed at (perhaps too great) length this somewhat caricatural commentary, it is because I wanted to bring to light some features of the life of science as lived in universes where it is possible to manifest a very high degree of incomprehension of competing works without incurring discredit; and also because, with some other writings in similar vein, it has been the source of a number of misreadings of my work which are very widespread in the world of the sciences of science.

1 The 'craft' of the scientist

The notion of the habitus is perhaps especially useful when one is seeking to understand the logic of a field such as the scientific field, in which the *scholastic illusion* operates with particular force. Just as the *lector*'s illusion led to the work of art being apprehended as an *opus operatum*, in a 'reading' ignorant of art (in Durkheim's sense) as 'pure practice without theory', so too the scholastic vision which seems to prevail especially in matters of science makes it impossible to know and recognize the truth of scientific practice as the product of a scientific habitus, a practical sense (of a very particular type). If there is one area where it can be assumed that agents act in accordance with conscious, calculated intentions, following consciously devised methods and programmes, it is indeed the domain of science. This scholastic vision is the basis of the logicist vision, one of the most successful manifestations of 'scholastic bias': just as iconological theory derived its interpretative principles from the *opus operatum*, the finished work of art, instead of attending to the work in progress and the *modus operandi*, so too a certain logicist epistemology sets up as the truth of scientific practice a norm of this practice derived *ex post facto* from completed scientific practice or, to put it another way, endeavours to deduce the logic of the practice from the logically consistent products of the practical sense.

To reintroduce the idea of the habitus is to set up as the principle of scientific practices, not a knowing consciousness acting in accordance with the explicit norms of logic and experimental method, but a 'craft', a practical sense of the problems to be dealt with, the appropriate ways of dealing with them, etc. In support of what I have just said, and to reassure you if you suppose that I am simply transposing to science my understanding of practice, to which scientific practice might be an exception, I will invoke the authority of a classic and much quoted text by Michael Polanyi (1951) – it is a much discussed theme and I could have cited many other authors – who points out that the criteria for evaluating scientific works cannot be completely articulated. There is always an implicit, tacit dimension, a conventional wisdom engaged in evaluating scientific works. This practical mastery is a kind of 'connoisseurship' which can only be communicated through example, and not through precepts (unlike methodology); it is not so different from the art of recognizing a good picture, or identifying its period and author, without necessarily being able to articulate the criteria that one is applying. 'Scientific research – in short – is an art' (Polanyi 1951: 57). Having said this, Polanyi is in no way opposed to the formulation of rules of verification and refutation, of measurement or objectivity, and he lauds the efforts made to make these criteria as explicit as possible. [Reference to practice is often inspired by a wish to denigrate intellectuality, reason; and this does not make it easy to assemble the theoretical instruments that one needs in order to understand practice. The new sociology of science often succumbs to this temptation of denigrating reason and one might say that, just as 'there is no great man in the eyes of his valet', so there is no great scientist – think of Pasteur – in the eyes of his sociologist … Social science is so difficult because, as Bachelard put it, errors come in pairs of complementary positions, so that one risks escaping one error only to fall into another, with logicism having as its opposite pole a kind of disenchanted 'realism'.]

But one can also draw support from the works of the new sociology of science, such as those of Lynch, who points to the discrepancy between what is said about scientific practice in books (of logic or epistemology) or in the protocols in which scientists report on what they have done, and what really happens in laboratories. The scholastic approach to scientific practice leads to the production of a kind of 'fiction'. Statements by researchers are remarkably like those of artists or sportspeople: they know full well how difficult it is to put practice, and the way to acquire it, into words. When they try to express their sense of correct procedure, they have little to call on beyond their past experience, which remains implicit and quasi-corporeal, and when they talk informally about their research, they describe it as a practice requiring experience, intuition, skill, flair, a 'knack', all things difficult to set down on paper, which can only really be understood and acquired by example and through personal contact with competent persons. Scientists, and especially chemists, often invoke the analogy with cooking and its recipes. And, indeed, as Pierre Laszlo (2000) shows, perfectly illustrating Polanyi's remarks, the chemistry laboratory is a place of manual work where things are 'manipulated', where scientists apply systems of practical schemes which are learned little by little by following laboratory protocols. In a general way, the competence of the lab scientist is to a large extent made up of a whole series of routines, mostly manual, demanding much dexterity and involving delicate instruments – dissolving, extraction, filtering, evaporation, etc.

Practice is always underestimated and under-analysed, and yet understanding it requires much theoretical competence, much more, paradoxically, than understanding a theory. One has to avoid reducing practices to the idea one has of them when one's only experience of them is logical. And, for lack of an adequate theory of practice, scientists are not necessarily able to invest in their descriptions of their practices the theory that would enable them to have and to give a real knowledge of these practices.

The analogy that some analysts draw between artistic practice and scientific practice is not without foundation, but within certain limits. The scientific field is, like other fields, the site of practical logics, but the difference is that the scientific habitus is a realized, embodied theory. A scientific practice has all the properties recognized in the most typically practical practices, such as sporting or artistic practices. But this does not prevent it from also being perhaps the supreme form of theoretical intelligence: it is, to parody the language of Hegel speaking of morality, 'a theoretical consciousness realized', that is to say, embodied, incorporated, in the practical state. Entering a laboratory is very like entering an artist's studio – it leads to the learning of a whole series of schemes and techniques. But the specificity of the scientist's 'craft' stems from the fact that this learning process consists in the acquisition of extremely complex theoretical structures which may moreover be encapsulated in formulae, especially mathematical ones, and which can be acquired rapidly thanks to this formalization. The difficulty of initiation into any scientific practice (whether quantum physics or sociology) lies in the fact that a double effort is required in order to master the knowledge theoretically but in such a way that this knowledge really passes into practice, in the form of a 'craft', 'knacks', an 'eye', etc., and does not remain in the state of a meta-discourse about practices. The 'art' of the scientist is indeed separated from the 'art' of the artist by two major differences: on the one hand, the importance of the formalized knowledge which is mastered in the practical state, owing in particular to formalization and formularization, and on the other hand the role of the instruments, which, as Bachelard put it, are formalized knowledge turned into things. In other words, a twenty-year-old mathematician can have twenty centuries of mathematics in his mind because formalization makes it possible to acquire accumulated products of non-automatic inventions, in the form of logical automatisms that have become practical automatisms.

The same is true as regards instruments: to perform a 'manipulation', one uses instruments that are themselves scientific conceptions condensed and objectivated in equipment functioning as a system of constraints, and the practical mastery that Polanyi refers to is made possible by an incorporation of the constraints of the instrument so perfect that one is corporeally bound up with it, one responds to its expectations; it is the instrument that leads. One has to have incorporated much theory and many practical routines to be able to fulfil the demands of a cyclotron.

We must pause for a moment to consider the question of the relationship between practice and method, which seems to me to be a particular form of the Wittgensteinian question of what it means to follow a rule. One does not act in accordance with a method, any more than one follows a rule, by a psychological act of conscious adherence, but essentially by letting oneself be carried along by a sense of – a feel for – the scientific game that is acquired through prolonged experience of the scientific game, with its *regularities* as much as its rules. These rules and regularities are constantly under-lined, either by express formulations (the rules governing the presen-tation of scientific texts, for example), or by indices embedded in the very functioning of the field, and most especially in the instruments (including mathematical tools) requiring the knack of the experienced experimenter.

A scientist is a scientific field made flesh, an agent whose cognitive structures are homologous with the structure of the field and, as a consequence, constantly adjusted to the expectations inscribed in the field. These rules and regularities, which 'determine', so to speak, the scientist's behaviour, exist as such – that is, as factors effectively capable of orienting scientists' practice in the direction of conformity with the demands of scientificity – only because they are perceived by scientists endowed with the habitus that makes them capable of perceiving and appreciating them, and both disposed and able to implement them. In short, the rules and regularities determine the agents only because the agents determine themselves by a *practical* act of cognition and recognition which confers their determining power on them, or, to put it another way, because these agents are so disposed (as a result of a specific effort of socialization) that they are sensitive to the injunctions they contain and prepared to respond meaningfully to them. It can be seen that it would no doubt be futile, in these conditions, to ask which is the cause and which the effect, and if it is even possible to distinguish between the causes of action and the reasons for acting.

Here one needs to turn back to the analyses of Gilbert and Mulkay (1984), describing scientists' efforts to present their work in 'formal' language, conforming to the prevailing rules of presentation and the official idea of science. In this case, they are likely to be aware of obeying a norm and one can no doubt speak of a real intention to follow the rule. But does it not also happen that they obey the concern to be seen to be 'in line' with the rule? In other words, consciously to close a perceived gap between the rule, perceived as such, and prac-tice, which, precisely by its non-conformity to the rule, calls for the explicit effort needed to 'regularize' it?

To summarize: the real principle of scientific practices is a system of largely unconscious, transposable, generative dispositions, which tends to generalize itself. This habitus takes specific forms depending on the speciality. Shifts from one discipline to another, from physics to chemistry in the nineteenth century, from physics to biology now, give an opportunity to observe the disparities between these systems: because contacts between sciences, like contacts between civilizations, are occasions when implicit dispositions have to be made explicit, in particular in the interdisciplinary groups that form around a new object, they would be a particularly favourable area for observing and objectivating these practical schemes. [Confrontations between specialists in different disciplines, and therefore with different training, owe many of their characteristics – effects of domination, misunderstandings, etc. – to the structure of the capital possessed by each side: in teams in which physicists and biologists are brought together, for example, the former bring strong mathematical competence, the latter a greater specific competence, both more 'bookish' and more practical, but the relationship, previously tilted towards the physicists, is increasingly moving in favour of the biologists, who, with their greater links with the economy and health, bring many new problems into play. Conversely, the most solid foundation for the unity of a discipline is no doubt a more or less homogeneous distribution of the capital held by the various members, even if secondary differences may remain, such as that between theorists and empiricists.]

These systems of dispositions vary according to the discipline, but also according to secondary principles such as educational or even social trajectories. It can therefore be assumed that habitus are principles of production of practices differentiated according to variables of sex and social origin and no doubt by country (through its educational system) and that, even in disciplines with a very large accumulated collective scientific capital, such as physics, an intelligible statistical relationship could be found between the scientific strategies of the various scientists and properties of social origin, trajectory, etc. [It can be seen in passing that the notion of the habitus can be understood both as a general principle of the theory of action – in opposition to the principles invoked by an intentionalist theory – and as a specific principle, differentiated and differentiating, of the actions of a particular category of agents, linked to particular conditions of training.]

So there are disciplinary habitus (which, because they are linked to education, are common to all products of the same mode of generation) and particular habitus linked to *trajectory* (both outside the field – social and educational origin – and within the field) and *position* within the field. [We know, for example, that, despite the autonomy linked to collective capital, the orientation towards this or that discipline, or, within a discipline, towards this or that specialty, or, within a specialty, towards this or that scientific 'style', is not independent of social origin: the social hierarchy of disciplines is not unrelated to the social hierarchy of origins.] It is no doubt possible to distinguish families of trajectories, with, in particular, the opposition between on the one hand the 'central' players, the orthodox, the continuers of normal science, and, on the other hand, the marginal, the heretics, the innovators, who are often situated on the boundaries of their disciplines (which they sometimes cross) or who create new disciplines on the boundaries of several fields.

I shall now attempt, with much hesitation, a very risky undertaking – endeavouring to characterize two scientific habitus and to relate them to the corresponding scientific trajectories. My main aim in so doing is to give an idea, or a programme, of what a refined sociology of science would have to do. If it appeared that one could discover any hint of a difference between scientists who work in domains where the accumulated collective capital and the degree of formalization are very great, and who initially possessed very similar educational capital – such as Pierre-Gilles de Gennes and Claude Cohen-Tannoudji, who entered the Paris École normale supérieure (ENS) at roughly the same time and were both consecrated, fifty years later, by a Nobel prize jury – then one might conclude that social (familial) habitus, translated into academic and scientific terms, has a non-zero explanatory efficacy. [Contrasted portraits of Pierre-Gilles de Gennes and Claude Cohen-Tannoudji can be found in Anatole Abragam's autobiography *Time Reversal* (1989).] It goes without saying, in my view, that the partial explicability of scientific strategies by social variables would in no way reduce the scientific validity of the scientific products. I do not have all the information that would be needed to delineate rigorously the contrasted portraits of the two oeuvres and I shall simply here contrast two 'styles', apprehended through indices that are no doubt very crude, and relate them to some equally crude indices of social origin and trajectory, aristocratic on the one hand, petit-bourgeois on the other. Whereas Claude Cohen-Tannoudji remained at the ENS, and continued a (great) tradition, that of atomic physics, Pierre-Gilles de Gennes left the ENS, to study objects on the boundary of physics and chemistry, condensed matter, with the physics of superconductivity, which at the time was also a 'noble' domain; then moved on to soft matter, liquid crystals, polymers, emulsions, a somewhat hybrid domain which may be perceived as less important. On the one hand, the academically most noble path, but also the most difficult one, concentrating the greatest stakes and the most fearsome competitors, and leading, after some great discoveries, such as Bose-Einstein condensation – which gave new life to the domain – to a major reference work, *Quantum Mechanics*, regarded as the Bible of the discipline; and on the other, a more risky, less 'academic' path, closer to applications and industry (with polymers, of considerable industrial and economic interest). Two trajectories, then, which appear as the projection of two different types of dispositions, two different types of relationship to the social world and the academic world.

To understand how social origins, and therefore the dispositions expressed in them – audacity, elegance and ease, or seriousness, conviction and investment – were gradually translated into these trajectories, one would have to examine for example whether the echoed image of itself that a particular habitus may receive in the regions in which it is engaged did not help, in each case, to foster these dispositions. The habitus, as I have said so many times, is not a destiny, and none of the contrasting dispositions that I have mentioned is inscribed, *ab ovo*, in the original habitus. A posture which might be perceived as a superficial lightness ('is it really serious?') may also be seen as a promising 'ease' if it has in some sense found its 'natural home', in other words a region of the field occupied by people predisposed by their position and their habitus to apprehend positively and appreciate favourably the behaviours in which this habitus is unveiled, revealed (in part also to itself), and so to reinforce it, confirm it and lead it to its full development, in the particular style that is characterized for example as economy of means, conceptual elegance, etc. The habitus manifests itself continuously, in oral examinations, in seminar presentations, in contacts with others, and, more simply, in a bodily hexis, a way of tilting the head, a posture of the body, which is its most directly visible transcription, and the social reception of these visible signs sends back to the person in question an image of himself which means that he feels authorized and encouraged, or not, in his dispositions, which, in other people, would be discouraged or forbidden.

I wanted to carry out this exercise, in the hope that I will one day be able extend it myself, with the collaboration of the scientists concerned, or that others will pursue it. It would require a systematic survey which would presuppose the collaboration of researchers in the natural sciences and the social sciences, one of the main functions of the sociologist being, in this case, to assist the scientists in the work of making explicit the practical schemes that underlay their decisive choices – the choice of this or that discipline, laboratory or journal. The effort to make these things explicit, a very difficult operation for those concerned if they were left to themselves, would be facilitated by methodical use of comparison, which would take on its full strength if, on the basis of a multiple correspondence analysis, it were possible to conduct it on the scale of the whole field, including the most distant points, but also, and especially, the closest ones.

2 Autonomy and the conditions of entry

I will start by reminding you of some of the points I made in my early article (Bourdieu 1975a), which said essentially what needed to be said but somewhat elliptically, so as to show that the notion of the field is perhaps primarily useful on account of the errors it enables one to avoid, in particular in constructing the object, and also inasmuch as it enables one to resolve a number of difficulties that the other approaches have raised. I shall also try to integrate some of the gains from recent theories and to draw out the new implications from the old model by making some additions and corrections.

I would first like to show in what way the notion of the field enables one to break away from some presuppositions that are tacitly accepted by most of those who have taken an interest in it. The first to be called into question is the idea of 'pure' science, perfectly autonomous and developing according to its internal logic. With it goes the idea of the 'scientific community', a notion regarded as self-evident which, through the logic of verbal automatisms, has become a kind of obligatory designation of the scientific world. Merton orchestrates the idea of 'community' with the theme of the 'communism' of scientists, and Warren Hagstrom's book (1965) defines the scientific community as a 'group whose members are united by a common objective and culture'. To speak of a field is to break with the idea that scientists form a unified, even homogeneous group.

The idea of the field also leads one to call into question the irenic vision of the scientific world, that of a world of generous exchanges in which all scientists collaborate towards the same end. This idealist vision which describes practice as the product of voluntary submission to an ideal norm is contradicted by the facts: what one observes are struggles, sometimes ferocious ones, and competitions within structures of domination. The 'communitarian' vision fails to grasp the very foundation of the scientific world as a universe of competition for the 'monopoly of the legitimate handling' of scientific goods, in other words and more precisely, of the correct method, the correct findings, the correct definition of the ends, objects and methods of science. And, as one sees when Edward Shils observes that in the 'scientific community' every element of the scientific tradition is subject to critical evaluation, this vision is thus led to describe as a voluntary accomplishment and a deliberate submission to an ideal norm what is in fact the product of submission to objective, anonymous mechanisms.

The notion of the field also destroys all kinds of common oppositions, starting with the one between consensus and conflict, and, while it sweeps away the naïvely idealist view of the scientific world as a community of solidarity or a 'kingdom of ends' (in the Kantian sense), it is also opposed to the no less partial view of scientific life as a 'war of all against all' that scientists themselves sometimes evoke (when for example they describe one or another among them as a 'killer'): scientists have things in common which in one respect unite them and in another respect separate them, divide them, set them against each other – ends, for example, even the most noble ones, such as finding the truth or combating error, and also everything that determines the competition and makes it possible, such as a common culture, which is also a weapon in scientific struggles. Scientists, like artists or writers, are united by the struggles that divide them, and even the alliances that may unite them always have something to do with the positions they occupy within these struggles.

Having said this, the notion of 'community' points to another important aspect of scientific life: all those who are engaged in a scientific field may, in certain conditions, equip themselves with instruments that enable them to function as communities, whose official function is to advocate and protect the ideal values of the profession of scientist. These are the learned societies, the 'corporate' institutions of defence and cooperation, whose operation, social composition and organizational structure (management etc.) have to be understood in terms of the logic of fields; there are also all the organizational forms that durably and permanently structure the practices of the agents and their interactions, such as the CNRS [Centre national de la recherche scientifique – the French national research council] or the laboratory, and one needs to secure the means of studying these institutions, while bearing in mind that they do not contain the principle of their own understanding and that, in order to understand them, one has to understand the positions within the field of those who belong to them. A disciplinary association (such as the Société française de biologie) will help to sustain, within the disciplinary field, the functioning of something like a community, managing part of the common interests and relying on common interests, the common culture, in order to function. But, to understand how it functions, one has to take account of the positions occupied within the field by those who belong to it and run it. It will then be found that some agents find in membership of these associations and in the defence of the common interests resources that the laws of functioning of the scientific field do not give them. This is linked to the existence of two principles of domination in the scientific field, temporal and intellectual, the temporal powers often being on the side of community logic, that is to say the common management of affairs, a minimal consensus, a minimum of basic common interests, international conferences, relations with other countries, or, in the event of serious conflict, the defence of the collective interests.

Most analysts ignore the relative autonomy of the field and pose the problem of the constraint exerted on the field (by religion, the state, etc.), of rules imposed by force. Barnes seeks to 'exorcize' the idea of the autonomy of science: he rejects the idea that science differs from other forms of culture in being as pure and 'undistorted', that is to say, autonomous; he aims to conduct a sociology that applies as well to true beliefs as to false beliefs inasmuch as they are the product of social forces (Barnes 1974). In fact, the field is subject to (external) *pressures* and contains *tensions*, in the sense of forces that act so as to drive apart, separate, the constituent parts of a body. To say that the field is relatively autonomous with respect to the encompassing social universe is to say that the system of forces that are constitutive of the structure of the field (tension) is relatively independent of the forces exerted on the field (pressure). It has, as it were, the 'freedom' it needs to develop its own necessity, its own logic, its own *nomos*.

One of the characteristics that most differentiate fields is their *degree of autonomy* and, related to this, the force and form of the *entry conditions* imposed on new entrants. We know for example that the literary field is characterized, relative to other fields, such as the bureaucratic field, the scientific field or legal field, by the fact that the entry conditions, measured in academic terms, are very low. (When one considers the scientificity of a field, one is referring to properties which all have to do with degree of autonomy. For example, the social sciences must endlessly reckon with external forces which hold back their 'take-off'.)

So I shall now try to describe this autonomy, then the logic and the factors of the process of autonomization and, finally, I shall try to examine what constitutes the conditions of entry in this particular case. Autonomy is not a given, but a historical conquest, endlessly having to be undertaken anew. This is easily forgotten in the case of the natural sciences, because their autonomy is inscribed both in the objectivity of the structures of the field and also in scientists' minds, in the form of theories and methods, incorporated and returned to the practical state.

Autonomy, in this field as in all others, was won by stages. The scientific revolution that started with Copernicus was completed, according to Joseph Ben-David, with the creation of the Royal Society in London: 'The institutional aim of that revolution – namely, the

establishment of science as a distinct intellectual activity, to be controlled only by its own norms – was accomplished in the seventeenth
century' (Ben-David 1991: 339). One of the most important factors in
this process, which Kuhn discusses in one of the essays in *The Essential Tension*, 'Mathematical versus experimental traditions in the
development of physical science' (1977: 31–65), was mathematization. And Yves Gingras, his article 'Mathématisation et exclusion,
socioanalyse de la formation des cités savantes' (2002), shows that
mathematization lies behind several convergent phenomena which all
tend to strengthen the autonomy of the scientific world and especially
physics (it is not certain that this phenomenon always and everywhere
has the same effects, particularly in the social sciences).

Mathematization first produces an effect of exclusion from the field
of discussion (Gingras recalls the resistance to the effect of exclusion
produced by the mathematization of physics – for example, Abbé
Nollet 'claimed the right to put forward his opinion'). With Newton
(I would add Leibniz), the mathematization of physics tended increasingly, from the mid-eighteenth century, to set up a very strong social
separation between professionals and amateurs, insiders and out-
siders. Mastery of mathematics (acquired in the training period)
became the price of entry and reduced not only the number of potential readers but also of potential producers (which, as will be seen, has
enormous consequences). 'The boundaries of the space were slowly
redefined in such a way that the potential readers were more and more
limited to the potential contributors, having the appropriate training.
In other words, mathematization contributed to the formation of
an autonomous scientific field' (Gingras 2001: 24). Faraday, for
example, suffered the exclusion effect of Maxwell's mathematics.
Separation implies closure, which produces censorship. Each researcher engaged in the field is subjected to monitoring by all the
others, and in particular by his most competent competitors, the
result being a control much more powerful than that of mere individual virtues or any deontology.

The second consequence of mathematization is the transformation
of the idea of explanation. It is by calculating that a physicist explains
the world, generating the explanations that he will then need to
confront by experimentation with the predicted outcomes as provided
by the experimental apparatus. If Kuhn had based his model of
revolution not, as he did, on the Copernican revolution, but on
Newton's, he would have seen that Newton was the first to provide
mathematical explanations which implied a change in physical theory.
Without necessarily taking a position on the corresponding ontology

(one can of course speak of action at a distance, etc.), he substituted a mathematical explanation for explanation by mechanical contact (as put forward by Descartes or Leibniz), which implied a redefinition of physics.

This leads to a third effect of mathematization, which can be called desubstantialization, in the terms of Cassirer's analysis in *Substance and Function*, to which Gingras also refers. Modern science substitutes functional relations, structures, for Aristotelian substances, and it is the logic of the manipulation of symbols that guides the physicist's hands towards the necessary conclusions. The use of abstract mathematical formulations weakens the tendency to conceive matter in substantial terms and leads to emphasis being placed on relational aspects. I am thinking here of a book by Michel Bitbol, *Mécanique quantique* (1996), which makes it possible to understand this process of the desubstantialization of physics by mathematics, and more precisely by probability calculation functioning as a 'predictive symbolism' (Bitbol 1996: 141). Calculation of probabilities makes it possible to provide predictions for subsequent measurements on the basis of initial measurements. Bitbol, who places himself in the tradition of Bohr, avoids reference to any reality, any ontological statement about the world: 'what is measured with instruments' serves as the basis for experiments that enable measurements to be predicted. Epistemology does not have to take a position on the reality of the world; it simply takes a position on the predictability of measurements which enables one to implement the calculation of probabilities on the basis of past measurements. Probability calculation or Hilbert's coordinate formalism, Bitbol goes on to say, are a way of communicating between physicists 'which avoids the need for the concept of a physical system on which measurements are made' (Bitbol 1996: 142). [The evolution of the notion of the field could no doubt be seen as an illustration of this process of 'desubstantialization', with, in the first stage, static fields – electrostatic or gravitational fields, which are identities subordinated to the particles that give rise to them, that is, possible, non-obligatory descriptions of the interaction of the particles; then, in a second stage, classical dynamic fields – the electromagnetic field – where the field has an existence of its own and can persist after the disappearance of the particles; and, finally, a third stage, quantum fields, quantum electrodynamics, in which the system of charges is described as a 'field operator'.]

The resulting process of autonomization also takes place in the objectivity of the social world, in particular through the creation of some quite extraordinary realities (we don't realize how extraordinary, because we are used to them) – namely, disciplines. The gradual institutionalization in universities of these relatively autonomous fields is the product of struggles for independence aimed at imposing the existence of new entities and the boundaries intended to delimit and protect them (battles over frontiers are often over the monopoly of a name, with all kinds of consequences, budget lines, posts, grants, etc.). In his book *Physics and the Rise of Scientific Research in Canada* (1991), Yves Gingras distinguishes, within the development of a scientific field, first, the emergence of a research practice, in other words, agents whose practice is based more on research than on teaching, and the institutionalization of research in universities through the creation of conditions conducive to the production of knowledge and the long-term reproduction of the group; and, secondly, the constitution of a group recognized as socially distinct and a social identity, either disciplinary, through the creation of scientific associations, or professional, with the creation of a corporation – the scientists provide themselves with official representatives to give them social visibility and defend their interests. This last process is not adequately described simply as 'professionalization': in fact, there are two practices of physics, one confined to universities, the other open to industry, where physicists are in competition with engineers, with, on the one hand, the construction of a scientific discipline, with its associations, meetings, journals and official representatives, and on the other, the delimitation of a 'profession' monopolizing access to titles and the corresponding posts. People often forget the duality of the scientific world, with on one side the researchers, affiliated to universities, and on the other the body of engineers which endows itself with its own institutions, pension funds, associations, etc. For example, in Britain after the First World War physicists became concerned about their social status and aware of their social non-existence; they created a representative organization, the Institute of Physics, and imposed a vision in which research is an integral part of the functions of a university.

The process of autonomization is linked to the rise in the implicit or explicit *price of entry*. This price of entry is competence, scientific capital (for example, as has just been seen, knowledge of mathematics, an ever more essential requirement), incorporated and turned into a 'sense of the game', but it is also the propensity to take part in the game, the *libido scientifica*, the *illusio*, the belief not only in the stakes but also in the game itself, the idea that the game is worth the candle, that it is worth playing. Being the products of education, competence and propensity are statistically linked because they develop in correlation (essentially in the course of education).

First, competence: this means not only mastery of existing knowledge, of the resources accumulated in the field (mathematics in particular), but also the fact of having incorporated all the theoretical-experimental (that is to say, cognitive and material) resources resulting from previous research, transforming them into a practical sense of the game, converting them into reflexes (Kuhn's 'essential tension' being inscribed in the fact that the tradition to be mastered in order to enter the game is the very condition for the revolutionary break). So the price of entry is competence, but competence as a theoretical-experimental resource 'embodied', turned into a sense of the game, in other words the scientific habitus as a practical mastery of several centuries of research and gains from research – in the form, for example, of a sense of what are the important, interesting problems, or an arsenal of theoretical and experimental schemes that can be applied, by *transfer*, to new domains.

What the scholastic taxonomies describe through a whole series of oppositions which come down to the distinction between the brilliant, the effortless, the fluent, and the serious, the laborious, the 'scholastic', is the relation of perfect adjustment to the expectations and demands of a field, which demands not only knowledge but a *relation to knowledge* capable of masking the fact that the knowledge has had to be acquired, learned (especially in the literary universe) or of manifesting that the knowledge is so perfectly mastered that it has become a natural automatism (as opposed to the bookish competences of the exam-passer who has a head full of formulae which he does not know how to use when faced with a real problem). In short, what the scientific field demands is a particular type of incorporated capital, and, in particular, a whole set of theoretical resources returned to the practical state, the state of practical sense (an 'eye', as it is put in the case of the artistic disciplines, or, as when Everett Hughes speaks of the 'sociological eye', sociology itself).

Each discipline (as a field) is defined by a particular *nomos*, a principle of vision and division, a principle of construction of objective reality irreducible to that of another discipline – in accordance with Saussure's formula, 'the point of view creates the object' (the arbitrariness of the 'disciplinary eye' as a constitutive principle is seen in the fact that it is most often expressed in the form of tautologies, with, for example, in sociology, 'explaining the social by the social', in other words explaining social things sociologically).

I now turn to the second dimension of the conditions of entry, the *illusio*, belief in the game, which implies, among other things, unconstrained submission to the imperative of disinterestedness. Steven Shapin, co-author with Simon Schaffer of a book on the air pump,

shows how the birth of the field coincided with the invention of a new
belief (Shapin and Schaffer 1985). Experiments were formerly conducted in the 'public rooms' of the private residences of 'gentlemen'.
Knowledge was confirmed as authentic, authenticated, accepted,
when it entered the public space, but a particular kind of public
space: it was the status of 'gentleman' that confirmed the validity of
the testimonies, and therefore the reliability and objectivity of the
experimental knowledge, because 'gentlemen' were presumed to be
free of any interest (unlike their servants, who were permitted to
attend experiments, 'gentlemen' were independent of authority and
money, autonomous). Valid testimony was a relation of honour between men of honour, between 'disinterested free men, gathered freely
around experimental phenomena and creating the fact attested'. 'Experimental trials' marked the shift from the private realm (aristocratic
houses had their public part and their private part) to the public space
of the Academies and, at the same time, from opinion to knowledge.
Thus the legitimacy of knowledge depends on a public presence in
some phases of the production of the knowledge.

But I would also to mention here an article in which Mario Biagioli
(1998), the author of some admirable works on Galileo, discusses the
effects of the pressure of external demands, which, in some areas of
research, threatens the disinterestedness of scientists or, more precisely, the specific interest in disinterestedness (as is seen in the area
of biomedicine, where because of the very high economic stakes and
under the pressure of a competitive, entrepreneurial environment,
there has been a sharp increase in multiauthorship and the development of a capitalist ethos). Biagioli discovers the tension between the
obligatory disinterestedness which is imposed by the cross-controls
exerted by the field on each of those engaged in it (to be in a scientific
field is to be placed in conditions in which one has an interest in
disinterestedness, not least because disinterestedness is rewarded) and
a strong social demand, economically sanctioned, which calls for
concessions. He points out the radical difference, in the area of
science, between 'intellectual property law and the reward system of
science', as I describe it in my analysis of symbolic capital: 'A new,
dramatic discovery that may warrant a Nobel Prize cannot be translated, in and of itself, into a patent or a copyright. ... The primary
currency of scientific credit is not money per se, but rewards assigned
through peer review (reputation, prizes, tenure, membership in societies, etc.) rather than transacted according to the logic of the
market.' This 'honorific credit' is personal and is not transferable
(scientific authorship cannot be a form of private property, and
cannot be transferred by contract or inheritance: I cannot bequeath

my symbolic capital). It is attached to the scientist's name and constructed as non-monetary. In short, what scientific virtue produces is a certain disposition, socially constituted, in relationship with a field that rewards disinterestedness and sanctions any lapses from this (in particular, scientific fraud).

In a general way, disinterestedness is not at all the product of a kind of 'spontaneous generation' or a gift of nature. It can be shown that, in the present state of the scientific field, it is the product of the action of the educational system and the family, which makes it a partly 'hereditary' disposition. For example, as one moves towards the educational institutions which train for the most disinterested careers, such as science – the École normale supérieure, for example, as opposed to the École Polytechnique or, a fortiori, to the École nationale d'administration or the École des hautes études commerciales – one finds a growing proportion of students from families belonging to the educational and scientific worlds.

There is a kind of structural ambiguity of the scientific field (and of symbolic capital) which could be the objective basis of what Merton called the 'ambivalence of scientists' with regard to claims of priority: the institution which sets a premium on priority (that is to say symbolic appropriation) also values disinterestedness and 'selfless dedication to the advancement of knowledge' (Merton 1973). The field imposes both 'selfish' competition – together with the sometimes frenetic interests that competition fosters, through for example the fear of being overtaken in one's discoveries – and disinterestedness.

This ambiguity no doubt also explains how it has been possible to describe the exchanges that take place in the scientific field on the model of gift exchange, with each researcher having, if Hagstrom is to be believed, to give the others the new information he has discovered, in order to receive their recognition in return (Hagstrom 1965: 16–22). In fact, the pursuit of recognition is always strongly denied, in the name of the ideal of disinterestedness – which will not surprise those who know that the economy of symbolic exchanges, of which the paradigm is gift exchange, is based on the obligatory denial of interest. The gift can – and, in a certain respect, must – be experienced as a generous act of oblation with nothing received in return, while masking, even from the person who performs it, the ambition of securing a power, a lasting hold over the recipient – in a word, the virtual power relation – that it contains (on this point I refer you to the analyses of the dual truth of the gift which I have put forward, particularly in *Pascalian Meditations* (1999a). And it could be shown that scientific capital has a similar ambiguity, as a power relation based on recognition.

Having indicated how the field has constituted itself, by setting up a control on entry and then constantly exercising that control through the very logic of its functioning, and without any transcendent normativity, one can derive a first consequence, which can be called normative, from this observation. The fact that producers tend to have as their clients only their most rigorous and vigorous competitors, the most competent and the most critical, those therefore most *inclined* and most *able* to give their critique full force, is for me the *Archimedean point* on which one can stand to *give a scientific account of scientific reason*, to rescue scientific reason from relativistic reduction and explain how science can constantly progress towards more rationality without having to appeal to some kind of founding miracle. There is no need to move outside history in order to understand the emergence and existence of reason in history. The closure upon itself of the autonomous field constitutes the historical principle of the genesis of reason and the exercise of its normativity. It is, it seems to me, because I have, quite modestly, constituted it as a historical problem – thus enabling (and forcing) myself to establish scientifically the fundamental law of the functioning of the scientific world – that I have been able to *resolve the problem* of the relationship between reason and history or of the historicity of reason, a problem as old as philosophy and one which, especially in the nineteenth century, has haunted philosophers.

Another consequence of the closure linked to autonomy is that the scientific field obeys a logic different from that of a political field. If one speaks, as Latour (1987) does, of 'non-differentiation between the political level and the scientific level' then one may well feel entitled to place scientific strategies on the same level as intrigues to win funding or scientific prizes, and to describe the scientific world as a universe in which results are won by the power of rhetoric and professional influence – as if the principle of actions were ambition backed up with strategic and warlike rhetoric and as if scientists turned their attention to this or that theme of research solely in order to climb up the professional ladder, as others manoeuvre to win the Nobel Prize by surrounding themselves with a wide and dense network.

It is true that, in the scientific field, strategies have two sides to them. They have a pure – purely scientific – function and a social function within the field, that is to say, in relation to the other agents engaged in the field: for example, a discovery may be a symbolic murder that is not necessarily intended as such (as is seen when, through a delay of a few days or even a few hours, a researcher who is overtaken loses the profit of a lifetime's research) and which is a secondary effect of the structural – distinctive – logic of the field. But I shall return to this point.

3   Scientific capital, its forms and distribution

Scientific power relations are power relations that are set up and exerted in particular through cognitive and communicative relations (Bourdieu 1991a, 2001b). Symbolic power of the scientific type can be exerted only on agents who possess the categories of perception necessary to know it and recognize it. It is a paradoxical (and, in a sense, heteronomous) power which presupposes the 'complicity' of the agent who undergoes it. But I should first recall the essential properties of symbolic capital. Symbolic capital is a set of distinctive properties which exist in and through the perception of agents endowed with the adequate categories of perception, categories which are acquired in particular through experience of the structure of the distribution of this capital within the social space or a particular social microcosm such as the scientific field. Scientific capital is a set of properties which are the product of acts of knowledge and recognition performed by agents engaged in the scientific field and therefore endowed with the specific categories of perception that enable them to make the pertinent distinctions, in accordance with the principle of pertinence that is constitutive of the *nomos* of the field. This *diacritical* perception is only accessible to those who possess sufficient incorporated cultural capital. To exist scientifically is to have a 'plus' in terms of the categories of perception prevailing within the field, that is to say, for one's peers ('to have contributed something'), to have distinguished oneself (positively) by a *distinctive contribution*. In scientific exchange, the scientist makes a 'contribution' for which he is recognized by acts of public recognition such as citation among the sources of the knowledge used. Thus scientific capital is the product of recognition by competitors (and an act of recognition brings capital to the extent that the person who makes it is himself autonomous and rich in specific capital).

Scientific capital functions as a symbolic capital of recognition that is primarily, sometimes exclusively, valid within the limits of the field (although it can be converted into other kinds of capital, economic capital in particular): a scientist's symbolic weight tends to vary with the distinctive value of his contributions and the *originality* that his competitor-peers recognize in his distinctive contribution. The notion of *visibility*, used in the American university tradition, accurately evokes the differential value of this capital which, concentrated in a

known and recognized name, distinguishes its bearer from the undifferentiated background into which the mass of anonymous researchers
merges and blurs (in accordance with the opposition form / background
which is at the centre of the theory of perception – hence no doubt the
particular productivity of metaphors of perception, the matrix of which
is the opposition brilliant / obscure, in most scholastic taxonomies).

Although closely linked to it, symbolic capital is not identical to
incorporated cultural capital, in other words the greater or lesser
proportion of the collectively accumulated and theoretically available
scientific resources that is appropriated and mastered by the various
agents engaged in the field. The position that a particular agent
occupies in the structure of the distribution of this capital, as perceived by agents endowed with the capacity to perceive it and appreciate it, is one of the principles of the symbolic capital imparted to
that agent, inasmuch as it helps to determine his distinctive value, his
rarity, and inasmuch as it is generally linked to his contribution to the
progress of research and his distinctive value.

Symbolic capital flows to symbolic capital. The scientific field gives
credit to those who already have it: the best-known names are the
ones who benefit most from the symbolic profits that are apparently
distributed equally among the co-signatories in the cases of multiple
authorship or joint discoveries by unequally famous people – even
when the best-known do not take the first place, thereby earning the
additional profit of being seen as disinterested in terms of the norms
of the field. [Although Harriet A. Zuckerman's observations on 'name-
ordering among authors of scientific papers' (1968) may seem to show the
contrary, in fact they only confirm the law of concentration that I have just
put forward: because they are assured of greater automatic visibility, Nobel
Prize winners can manifest an appropriate disinterestedness by declining the
first place. But I shall not repeat here in detail the demonstration I made in my
1975 article (Bourdieu 1975a).]

The peer recognition that characterizes the field tends to produce an
effect of closure. Symbolic power of the scientific kind can be exerted
more widely, among 'lay persons' (as a power to make them see and
believe), only if it has been ratified by other scientists – who tacitly
control access to the 'public', particularly through the 'populariza-
tion' of science. [Political capital is also a symbolic capital of knowledge and
recognition or reputation, but it is won in the wider social field in accordance
with the logic of the plebiscite.]

The structure of the power relation that constitutes the field is
defined by the structure of the distribution of the two kinds of capital
(temporal and scientific) that are effective in the scientific field.

Because the autonomy is never total and because the strategies of the agents engaged in the field are inseparably scientific and social, the field is the site of two kinds of scientific capital: a capital of strictly scientific authority, and a capital of power over the scientific world which can be accumulated through channels that are not purely scientific (in particular, through the institutions it contains) and which is the bureaucratic principle of temporal powers over the scientific field such as those of ministers and ministries, deans and vice-chancellors or scientific administrators (these temporal powers tend to be more national, linked to national institutions, particularly those that govern the reproduction of the corps of scientists – such as Academies, committees, research councils, etc. – whereas scientific capital is more international).

It follows that the more autonomous a field is, the more the hierarchy according to the distribution of scientific capital is differentiated, even to the extent of taking an opposite form to that of the hierarchy by temporal capital (in some cases, such as the humanities and social science faculties that I studied in *Homo Academicus* (1988a), one finds a chiastic structure, with the distribution of temporal powers presenting an inverted form of the distribution of specific, strictly scientific power).

Judgements of scientific works are contaminated by knowledge of the position of the authors in the social hierarchies (and the more heteronomous the field is, the more this is the case). Thus Cole and Cole show that, among physicists, frequency of citation depends on the university to which a scientist is attached, and it is known that a researcher's symbolic capital, and therefore the reception of his work, depends in part on the symbolic capital of his laboratory. Constructivist microsociology fails to observe this; the structural constraints that bear on practices and strategies cannot be grasped at the microsociological level, that is, on the scale of the laboratory, because they are linked to the position of the laboratory within the field.

The logic of scientific struggles cannot be understood unless one takes into account the duality of the principles of domination. For example, in order to be pursued, the sciences require two types of resources, strictly scientific ones, which are for the most part incorporated, and the financial resources needed to buy or build equipment (such as the Berkeley cyclotron) or to pay staff, or administrative resources, such as posts; and, in the competition among them, researchers must always struggle to win their specific means of production in a field where the two kinds of scientific capital are effective.

The concessions that scientists have to make, individually or collectively, to activities oriented towards the search for economic resources – grants, contracts, posts, etc. – varies with the dependence of their scientific activity on these resources (and, secondarily, with their position in the hierarchy of the laboratory). It is zero, low or secondary in disciplines like mathematics or history but very strong in disciplines like physics or sociology. And the bureaucratic agencies responsible for overseeing the distribution of resources, in France the ministries or the CNRS, may – through the intermediary of scientific administrators or committees who are not necessarily best placed to do it *scientifically* – arbitrate in scientific conflicts between researchers.

The criteria of assessment are always at stake in the field and there is always a struggle over the criteria that enable the struggles (or 'controversies') to be settled. The power that scientific administrators exert over scientific fields, and which, whatever their intentions, is far from being governed by strictly scientific considerations (especially in the social sciences), can always exploit the internal divisions within the fields. And, in these areas as elsewhere, what I call the law of Zhdanovism – the law that those poorest in specific capital, in other words those least eminent on scientific criteria, tend to appeal to external powers to enhance their strength, and even sometimes to triumph, in their scientific struggles – comes into play.

Why is it important to bring to light the structure of the field? Because, by constructing the objective structure of the distribution of the properties attached to individuals or institutions, one acquires an instrument for forecasting the probable behaviours of agents occupying different positions within that distribution. For example, phenomena to which the 'new sociology of science' has drawn attention, such as the circulation and the process of consecration and universalization of scientific works, depend on the positions occupied in the structure of the field by the scientists concerned. Indeed, it can be posited (and it is observed) that the space of positions governs (in terms of probabilities) the homologous space of position-takings, that is to say, strategies and interactions. (This hypothesis puts an end to the distinction that some people make between the science of scientists and the science of scientific works.) Knowledge of the professional interests (linked to position and dispositions) that inform preferences can explain the choices made between different possibles: for example, in the nineteenth-century struggles between chemists and physicists, the latter, strong in physical and mathematical capital but knowing little of chemistry, were often led into errors and cul-de-sacs.

The structure of the scientific field is defined, at every moment, by the state of the power relations between the protagonists in the struggle, in other words by the structure of the distribution of the specific capital (in its different kinds) that they have been able to accumulate in earlier struggles. On the basis of each scientist's position within it, the structure assigns to him his scientific strategies and position-takings and their objective chances of success. These position-takings are the product of the relationship between a position in the field and the dispositions (the habitus) of its occupant. Every scientific choice – the area of research, the methods used, the place of publication, the choice, well described by Hagstrom (1965: 100), of rapid publication of partially verified findings or later publication of fully checked findings – is also a social strategy of investment oriented towards maximization of the specific, inseparably social and scientific profit offered by the field and determined by the relationship between position and dispositions that I have just set out.

In other words, knowledge of an agent's pertinent properties, and therefore of his position in the structure of the distribution, and of his dispositions, which are generally closely correlated with his properties and his position, makes it possible to predict (or at least understand) his specific position-takings (for example, the type of science he will pursue – 'normal' and reproductive, or eccentric and risky). If one could ask a sample of all French scientists a dozen questions on the one hand about their social origin, their education, the posts they have held, etc., and on the other about the type of science they do (questions which in this case would be very difficult to draw up and which would require a long preliminary survey), I think it would be possible to establish statistically significant relationships, similar in type to those I have established in other areas.

The relationship between the space of positions and the space of position-takings is not one of mechanical reflection: the space of positions exerts an effect on position-takings only through the habitus of the agents who apprehend that space, their position within it and the perception that the other agents involved in that space have of all or part of the space. The space of positions, when perceived by a habitus adapted to it (competent, endowed with a sense of the game), functions as a *space of possibles*, the range of possible ways of doing science, among which one has to choose; each of the agents engaged in the field has a practical perception of the various realizations of science, which functions as a *problematic*. This perception, this vision, varies according to the agents' dispositions, and is more or less complete, more or less extensive; it may rule out some sectors, disdaining them as uninteresting or unimportant (scientific revolu-

tions often have the effect of transforming the hierarchy of importance). The relationship between the space of possibles and dispositions can function as a system of censorship, excluding some
directions and means of research de facto without even stating any
restrictions. This narrowing effect is strongest for those agents who
have least symbolic capital and specific cultural capital (some
researchers may be led to rule out as impossible – 'not made for me'
– choices which may appear quite natural to others).

To have a space of mathematical possibles that is recognized as
mathematical by other mathematicians, you have to be a mathematician. But this space will vary according to the habitus of the mathematician in question, his specific competence, where he was trained,
etc. – and dispositions are one of the mediations of the effect of
the space of possibles on dispositions. And so, it is clear, in sociology,
causalities are always very complex: in order to be subject to an effect
of the field of mathematics, you have to be mathematically 'predisposed'. In other words, someone who is determined contributes to
his own determination, but through properties, such as dispositions
or capacities, that he has not determined. The choice of this or that
thesis subject, or the preference given to this or that branch of physics
or chemistry, bring into play two forms of determination: on the side
of the agent, his trajectory, his career, and, on the side of the field,
the objective space, structural effects which act on the agent in so far
as he is constituted in such a way as to be 'sensitive' to these effects
and therefore to make his own contribution to the effect that is
exerted on him. [This is said – without entering into philosophical discussions
on determinism and freedom – to remind philosophers and sociologists who
like to see themselves as philosophers that what we say is often more complicated than what they say about what we say – and perhaps even more than
what they say in the most complicated things that they believe they think about
freedom.]

The perception of the space of positions, which is both a cognition
and recognition of symbolic capital and a contribution to the constitution of this capital (through judgements based on indices such as
place of publication, the quality and quantity of notes, etc.), makes it
possible to orientate oneself in this field. When apprehended by a
well-constituted habitus, the various positions that are realized are so
many 'possibles', so many possible ways of doing what the agent who
perceives them does (such as physics or biology), possible ways of
doing science that are either already realized, or still to be realized,
but called for by the structure of already actualized possibles. A field
contains potentialities, a probable future, which a habitus adapted to
the field is able to anticipate. The physical world has immanent

tendencies, and the same is true of the social world. Science aims to establish the state of the world and consequently the immanent tendencies of that world, the probable future of that world, what cannot happen (the impossible) or what is more or less likely to happen (the probable) or even – but it is much more rarely in a position to do so – what must necessarily happen (the certain). To have knowledge of the structure is to acquire the means of understanding the state of the positions and the position-takings, but also the probable evolution, the future, of those positions and position-takings. In short, as I constantly repeat, analysis of the structure, the statics, and analysis of change, the dynamics, are indissociable.

The statics and the dynamics are inseparable, with the principle of the dynamics lying in the statics of the field, in the power relations that define it: the field has an objective structure that is nothing other than the structure of the distribution (in both the statistical and economic senses of the word) of the pertinent and therefore efficacious properties, assets that are effective within this field (here, scientific capital), and the power relations constitutive of this structure – which means to say that properties, which can be treated as logical properties, distinctive features making it possible to divide and classify (by contrasting and grouping, as one must in order to construct the structure of the distribution), are simultaneously stakes – possible objects of appropriation – and weapons – possible instruments for use in struggles to appropriate – for the groups which divide or assemble around them. The space of properties is also a field of struggles for appropriation.

When one uses a statistical technique such as correspondence analysis, one creates a multidimensional space in which both the properties and the holders of the properties distribute themselves, through a classificatory operation that makes it possible to characterize the structure of that distribution; but one only has to change the definition of these properties to consider them no longer as distinctive features in a classificatory taxonomy serving to differentiate agents and properties in a static space but as assets in the struggle within the field (for example, the fact of being long-established, or having published many Nobel Prize winners appears from this point of view as one of the foundations of the symbolic capital of a publishing house – Bourdieu 1999b), or, more precisely, as powers defining the foreseeable future of the game that will be played out among agents possessing unequal assets from the point of view of the definition of the game.

To represent the different kinds of power (or capital), one can use the metaphor of piles of tokens of different colours, which are the materialization both of the gains won in earlier phases of the game and weapons capable of being used in the subsequent rounds, in other words a kind of synthesis of the past and future of the game. It can be seen that to describe rigorously a state of the game, that is to say, the distribution of the winnings and assets, is also to describe the probable future of the game, the different players' probable chances of gain, and their probable strategies, given the state of their resources (assuming, that is, a strategy adjusted in practice to the chances of gain, reasonable rather than rational – as is the strategy of the habitus).

4   A regulated struggle

Agents, with their systems of dispositions, their respective competence, their capital, their interests, confront one another within the space of a game, the field, in a struggle to impose recognition of a form of cognition (an object and a method), thereby helping to conserve or transform the field of forces. A small number of agents and institutions concentrate sufficient capital to take the lead in appropriating the profits generated by the field – to exercise power over the capital held by other agents, the smaller holders of scientific capital. This power over capital is in fact exerted through power over the structure of the distribution of the chances of profit. The dominant players impose by their very existence, as a universal norm, the principles that they engage in their own practice. This is what is called into question by revolutionary innovation, which overthrows the structure of the distribution of the chances of profit, thus reducing the profits of those whose profits are linked to the old structure. A major scientific innovation may destroy whole swathes of research and researchers as a side-effect, without being inspired by the slightest intention of doing damage – I point this out to counter the cynical vision that may be suggested by analysis of scientific strategies as ways of 'competing', inspired by the desire to be first or to triumph over one's opponents. It is not surprising that innovations are not well received, that they arouse formidable resistance which may resort to defamation – a very effective weapon against a capital which, like symbolic capital, is *fama*, reputation, etc.

The dominant players impose de facto as the universal standard of the scientific value of scientific productions the principles that they themselves consciously or unconsciously engage in their practices, particularly in their choice of objects, methods, etc. They are set up as models, exemplary realizations of scientific practice, a realized ideal, incarnated norms; their own practice becomes the measure of all things, the right way to do science which discredits all other ways. They consecrate certain objects by investing in them and, through the very objects of their investments, they tend to act on the structure of the chances of profit, and so on the profits secured by the various investments. [Thus the CNRS is now borrowing the structures and, perhaps most significantly, the vocabulary of American science, imposing, as if it were self-evident, the idea of a research 'programme' or institutional models like the 'National Science Fund' (generally through the intermediary of personalities who, having been consecrated by the USA, reproduce the model that has consecrated them as the best or the only possible model).]

Revolutionaries, rather than simply playing within the limits of the game as it is, with its objective principles of price formation, transform the game and the principles of price formation. For example, one way of changing the prevailing mode of price formation is to change the mode of formation of the producers. This is what explains why struggles over the higher education system can be so violent (as one discovers as soon as one takes part in a committee on curricula, a quite fascinating experimental situation: I have seen people who, within a year of their retirement, with seemingly no direct interest in the matter, nonetheless engaged – to preserve an hour of Russian, geography or philosophy in the time-table – in battles aimed at perpetuating a whole system of beliefs, or rather, investments, by perpetuating the structure of the educational system).

Struggles over priority often pit a scientist who has discovered a simple fact, often an anomaly in terms of current knowledge, against a scientist who, with the aid of more advanced theoretical equipment, has constituted it as a scientific fact, a component in a new way of understanding the world. Epistemological wars are often of this type and take place between contestants endowed with different social properties predisposing them to feel affinity with one side or the other. One of the things at stake in epistemological struggles is always the valorization of one kind of scientific capital, that of the theorist or the experimenter for example (each contestant being inclined to defend the kind of capital with which he is particularly endowed).

The definition of what is at stake in the scientific struggle is one of the things at stake in the scientific struggle. The dominant players are those who manage to impose the definition of science that says that the most accomplished realization of science consists in having, being and doing what they have, are and do. That is why one constantly comes up against the antinomy of legitimacy: in the scientific field as elsewhere, there is no authority to legitimate the sources of legitimacy.

Scientific revolutions overthrow the hierarchy of the social values attached to the various forms of scientific practice, and therefore the social hierarchy of the various categories of scientists. One of the particularities of scientific revolutions is that they introduce a radical transformation while conserving the previous achievements. So they are revolutions that conserve past gains – without being conservative revolutions aimed at overthrowing the present to restore the past. They can only be performed by people who are in a sense specific capitalists, that is to say, people capable of mastering all the wealth of the tradition.

Scientific revolutions have the effect of transforming the hierarchy of importances: things considered unimportant may be reactivated by a new way of doing science, and, conversely, whole sectors of science may be overtaken, rendered obsolete. The struggles within the field are struggles to be or remain contemporary. Someone who introduces a new legitimate way of doing things shakes the power relations and introduces time. If nothing happened, there would be no time; the conservative agents would like to abolish time, to eternize the present state of the field, the state of the structure that is favourable to their interests because they occupy the dominant positions within it, whereas the innovators, without even seeking to 'compete' with anyone, introduce change by their mere intervention and bring about the specific temporality of the field. It follows that each field has its own time. A single chronology tends to impose a false unilinearity on different temporalities, the independent series corresponding to the different fields, which may indeed sometimes coincide, particularly when historical crises have the effect of synchronizing fields that have different histories and different temporalities.

I have so far spoken as if the subject of the scientific struggle were exclusively an individual, an individual scientist. In fact it can also be a discipline or a laboratory. We must consider for a moment the notion of a discipline. In ordinary usage, one may speak indifferently – referring to very different levels of the division of scientific labour – of a discipline or a subfield or a specialty (for example, the term 'discipline' will be used to refer to chemistry as a whole, or organic chemistry, physical chemistry, physical organic chemistry, quantum chemistry, etc.). Daryl E. Chubin distinguishes (Nye 1993: 2) the discipline (e.g. physics), the subfield (high-energy or particle physics), the specialty (weak interactions) and the subspecialty (experimental studies versus theoretical studies).

A discipline is a relatively stable and delimited field, and is therefore relatively easy to identify: it has an academically and socially recognized name (meaning one that is found, in particular, in library classifications, such as sociology as opposed to 'mediology', for example); it is inscribed in institutions, laboratories, university departments, journals, national and international fora (conferences), procedures for the certification of competences, rewards systems and prizes.

A discipline is defined by possession of a collective capital of specialized methods and concepts, mastery of which is the tacit or implicit price of entry to the field. It produces a 'historical transcendental', the disciplinary habitus, a system of schemes of perception and appreciation (where the incorporated discipline acts as a censorship). It is characterized by a set of socio-transcendental conditions, constitutive of a style. [A parenthesis on the notion of style: the products of the same habitus are marked by a unity of style (lifestyle, the manner or 'signature' of an artist). In the tradition of the sociology of science, the theme of style is found in the work of Mannheim and also Ludwik Fleck (1979), who speaks of 'styles of thought', that is to say, a 'tradition of shared assumptions', largely invisible and never questioned, and also of a 'thought collective', a community of people who regularly exchange thoughts: thoughts compatible with the fundamental assumptions of the collective are integrated, the others are rejected. We thus have a series of usages very close to one another, which are valid sometimes for a discipline as a whole, sometimes for a group, a thought collective which shares a body of knowledge and presuppositions about methodology, observation, acceptable hypotheses and the important problems – Ian Hacking (1992: 31) also refers to 'closed systems of research practice'.] This notion of 'style' is important at least in order to designate, to point to, a property of the various sciences, or disciplines, that has been crushed, eclipsed, in all reflection on science, by the fact that physics and, more precisely, quantum physics has been set up as the sole model of scientificity, in the name of a social privilege converted into an epistemological privilege by epistemologists and philosophers, who were ill-equipped to grasp the effects of social imposition that were exerted on their thinking.

The boundaries of the discipline are protected by a more or less codified, strict and high cost of entry; they are more or less sharply defined, and sometimes at issue in struggles with the neighbouring disciplines. There may be intersections between disciplines, some empty, others full, which offer the possibility of extracting ideas and information from a large or not so large number and range of sources. (Innovation in the sciences is often engendered in the intersections.)

The notion of the scientific field is important because it reminds one, on the one hand, that there is a minimum unity of science and, on the other hand, that the various disciplines occupy positions in the *(hierarchized) space of disciplines* and that what happens in them partly depends on these positions. To turn first to the question of unity: the scientific field can be described as a set of local fields (disciplines) which have in common some interests (for example the interest in rationality, against irrationalism, anti-science, etc.) and some minimum principles. Among the *unifying principles* of science, I think one has to make a very substantial place for what Terry Shinn (2000) calls 'stock instruments' (the ultracentrifuge, Fourier transform spectroscopy, the laser, the scintillation counter), 'generic instruments', 'epistemic things', which constitute a 'coagulated form of theoretical knowledge' (Shinn 2000), in which one should also include all rationalized, formalized, standardized forms of thought such as mathematics, capable of functioning as instruments of discovery, and the rules of experimental method. This scientific capital of standardized procedures, tried and tested models, recognized protocols that researchers borrow and combine to devise new theories or new experimental devices (with originality often consisting in a new combination of known elements), acts as a unifying factor and an antidote against centrifugal forces by imposing the incorporation of the rules (protocols) governing its use. Another unifying principle is no doubt the 'demonstration effect' which is exerted at each moment by the dominant science and which is the basis of borrowings between sciences.

A discipline is defined not only by intrinsic properties, but also by properties it owes to its position in the (hierarchized) space of disciplines. One of the most important principles of differentiation among the disciplines is the size of the capital of collective resources it has accumulated (in particular, theoretical-formal resources) and, correlatively, its degree of autonomy with respect to external (political, religious or economic) constraints. I will simply point out, without pursuing this, that there are two principles of differentiation / hierarchization among disciplines, the temporal principle and the strictly scientific principle.

To illustrate the effect of scientific, theoretical-formal resources, I shall briefly mention the relationship between physics and chemistry, as analysed by Nye (1993) and by Pierre Laszlo in his book *Miroir de la chimie* (2000). The opposition between physics and chemistry reappears at all levels of differentiation, in particular between mechanical physics, based on axiomatic and mathematical foundations, and a simple taxonomic and classificatory science, based on descriptive and empirical foundations. Pierre Laszlo evokes the experience of this objective relationship when he uses the phrase 'Lavoisier syndrome' (2000: 243) to describe chemists' embarrassment at calling themselves chemists: Lavoisier, the great eighteenth-century chemist, preferred to call himself a physicist. Chemistry, this descriptive and empirical science, concerned with practical, applied tasks (fertilizers, medicines, glass, insecticides) and using recipes (hence the analogy with cooking), is always described as a handmaid (Nye 1993: 3, 57). Laszlo refers to the 'childish, ludic aspect of chemistry' (2000: 243), which, like the other features already mentioned, takes its place in a homology with the opposition between the masculine and the feminine (which reappears very clearly in the opposition between theoretical physics and organic chemistry – Nye 1993: 6–7). In the early 1930s, a significant migration of physicists (London, Oppenheimer) into chemistry favoured the emergence among chemists of a 'molecular physics', linked to physics, with its own journals, and rebaptized in accordance with the dominant definition.

It seemed to me important to bring in the question of the discipline because disciplinary struggles can be a factor of scientific change through a whole series of effects, of which I will give just one example, described by Ben-David and Collins in a classic article on what has been called 'role-hybridization'. This hybridization, 'fitting the methods and techniques of the old role to the materials of the new one, with the deliberate purpose of creating a new role', occurs when field A (e.g. physiology) offers competitive advantages over field B (e.g. philosophy) and has lower status (Ben-David and Collins 1966): 'Mobility of scholars from one field to another will occur when the chances of success (i.e., getting recognition, gaining a full chair at a relatively early age, making an outstanding contribution) in one discipline are poor, often as a result of overcrowding in a field where the number of positions is stable. In such cases, many scholars will be likely to move to any related field in which the conditions of competition are better. In some cases, this will mean that they move into a field with a standing relatively lower than their original field. This creates the conditions for role conflict' (1966: 460). The scientist resolves the conflict linked to loss of a higher intellectual and possibly social status 'by innovating, that is, fitting the methods and techniques of the old role to the new materials of the new one, with the deliberate purpose of creating a new role'. This is done by means of a 'role-hybridization in which physiological methods will be applied to the material of philosophy (at their most adjacent point, psychology) in order to differentiate the innovator from the more traditional practitioners of the less respected discipline' (1966: 460). In short, once one discards the inadequate language of 'role conflict' and 'role-hybridization' and the philosophy of action it implies, it can be said (and it will be clear, I hope, that this not just a change in vocabulary) that this phenomenon appears when the representatives of a dominant discipline (philosophy in the cases of Fechner or Durkheim) move into a dominated discipline (psychology or sociology), suffering a loss of capital which in a sense obliges them to enhance the status of the discipline they have invaded by importing the gains of the discipline from which they come.

But constructing a discipline may also be the objective of a collective undertaking by agents aiming to secure the economic and social means of achieving a great scientific project, nothing less than discovering the 'secret of life' in the case in point. I would like to discuss very briefly – one ought really to go into all the details – the history of the 'phage workers', a group with a distinctive culture and a normative structure which acted as factors of integration, especially for the students trained by the group (Mullins 1972). It is an exemplary story which shows the theoretical and practical mistake made by those who think that the study of laboratories yields the principles of calculated strategies of 'self-aggrandizement' and 'political moves' in the scientific universe. It is clear from it that while there is a whole organizational effort of network building, etc., it all takes place in accordance with a logic which is not at all that of intention, calculation, or, to put it in a word, cynicism. First came a 'paradigm group' of people interested in the same research problem which constituted a bank of potential contacts. Then real relationships were set up through a 'network for communications' which grew through successive co-options. Slowly a real 'cluster' emerged, under the leadership of Max Delbrück, who organized the 'summer phage course'. Recognition as a group was based on the existence of a common intellectual style (a central dogma) and a social life (the summer course) and also, of course, on the first discoveries. A decisive role was played by the charisma of the leader, who, although he made many mistakes (for example, in trying to divert Watson from chemistry), was vindicated in his choice of the 'phage problem' and his aim of finding the 'secret of life'. The move from a cluster to a speciality was facilitated by the American university tradition of decentralization and competition: 'Molecular biology achieved the status of a department in the early 1960s.' In short, success was marked by the routinization of charisma. It is also clear that the rise or fall of a discipline cannot be understood unless one takes account both of its intellectual history and its social history, moving from the social

characteristics of the leader and his initial circle to collective properties of the group, such as its social attraction and its capacity to recruit
students.

It is because the scientific field is, in some respects, a field like others,
but one which obeys a specific logic, that it is possible to understand,
without appealing to any form of transcendence, how it can be the
historical site where trans-historical truths are produced. The first and
probably most fundamental of the distinctive properties of the scientific
field is, as we have seen, its (more or less total) closure, which means
that each researcher tends to have no other audience than the researchers most capable of listening to him but also of criticizing and even
refuting and disproving him. The second, which gives its particular
form to the censorship effect implied in that closure, is the fact that the
scientific struggle, unlike the artistic struggle, is aimed at the monopoly
of the scientifically legitimate representation of the 'real' and that
researchers, in their confrontation, tacitly accept the *arbitration of
the 'real'* (as produced by the theoretical and experimental equipment
actually available at the moment in question). Everything takes place as
if, adopting an attitude close to what the phenomenologists called the
'natural attitude', researchers tacitly agreed on the project of giving a
realist representation of the real; or, more precisely, tacitly accepted the
existence of an objective reality by taking upon themselves the project
of seeking and stating the truth of the world and agreed to be criticized,
contradicted, refuted, in the name of reference to the real, which is
constituted as the arbiter of research.

[This ontological postulate presupposes another one, the idea that there is
meaning, an order, a logic, in short something to be understood in the world,
including in the social world (as opposed to what Hegel called 'the atheism
of the moral world'); that one cannot say whatever one likes about the
world ('anything goes', in Feyerabend's phrase), because 'anything and everything' is not possible in the world. Not without some surprise, one finds
a perfect expression of this postulate in Frege: 'If everything were in continual
flux, and nothing maintained itself fixed for all time, there would no longer
be any possibility of getting to know anything about the world and everything
would be plunged in confusion' (Frege 1953: VII). This postulate, which has
not always been accepted for the natural world, remains contested – particularly in the name of the denunciation of 'determinism' – as regards the social
world.]

If sociological analysis of the functioning of the scientific field in no
way condemns one to a radical relativism, if one can and must
acknowledge that science is a thoroughly historical social fact without
concluding that its productions are relative to the historical and social

conditions of their emergence, this is because the 'subject' of science is not an integrated collective (as Durkheim and the Mertonian tradition supposed), but a field, and a very particular one, in which the power relations and relations of struggle among the agents and institutions are subject to the specific laws (of dialogue and argument) flowing from the two closely interrelated fundamental properties which I set out earlier: closure (or competition among peers) and the arbitration of the real. Logic itself, logical necessity, is the social norm of a particular category of social universes, scientific fields, and it is exerted through the constraints (especially the censorships) socially instituted in these universes.

To ground this proposition, one has to call into question a whole set of habits of thought, such as for example the tendency to perceive the relation of knowledge as a relationship between a singular scientist and an object. The subject of science is not the singular scientist but the scientific field, as a universe of objective relationships of regulated communication and competition that are regulated in terms of argumentation and verification. Scientists are never the 'singular geniuses' that hagiographic history makes of them: they are collective subjects which, in the form of incorporated collective history, actualize all the relevant history of their science – I am thinking for example of Newton or Einstein – and who work within collectives with instruments that are themselves objectified collective history. In short, science is an immense collective construction apparatus, used collectively. In a very autonomous scientific field, where the collective capital of accumulated resources is enormous, it is the field that 'chooses' the habitus capable of realizing its own tendencies – which does not mean that habitus are unimportant, inasmuch as they determine the orientation of individual trajectories within the space of possibles offered by a state of the field – whereas, in a field whose autonomy is constantly threatened – such as the field of sociology, which interests many people who would like to make it work in their service, etc. – habitus make a large contribution, unless particular vigilance is exerted, towards orienting practices.

The scientific struggle also owes its specificity (and this could be the third principle of differences with respect to the artistic struggle, itself characterized, in its most advanced stages, by closure) to the fact that the competitors for the monopoly of the legitimate representation of objective reality ('legitimate' meaning being capable of being recognized, validated – or, better, *homologated*, in the strong sense of the Greek root – in the present state of the instruments of communication, knowledge and criticism) have available to them an immense collective stock of equipment for theoretical construction and empirical verification or falsification which all participants in the competition are required to master. (I could, here again, invoke Terry Shinn: science is more and more dependent on 'research technology', which increasingly tends to become autonomized and become a discipline, offering new possibilities to the other disciplines, in accordance with the logic of its own development.) This equipment steadily grows through the advances in research, advances in knowledge of the object which are inseparable from advances in the instruments of knowledge.

[It takes less time to appropriate the resources accumulated in the objectified state (in books, instruments, etc.) than it took to accumulate them, which (together with the division of labour) is one of the reasons for the cumulativity of science and scientific progress. If a twenty-year-old mathematician can sufficiently master the historical gains of his discipline to contribute something new, this is partly due to the virtues of formalization and the generative condensation that it allows. Leibniz was aware of this phenomenon when he defended against Descartes the role of what he called *evidentia ex terminis*, the self-evidence that springs from the very logic of algebraic logical formulae, their transformations and developments, which he set against Cartesian self-evidence (especially in its independence of the fluctuations of intelligence or attention), which it enables one to dispense with.]

5 History and truth

Objectivity is a social product of the field which depends on the presuppositions accepted in the field, particularly as regards the legitimate way of settling conflicts (for example, coherence between facts and theory or replicability). The principles of logic and experimental method are constantly called into question when they are implemented in the transactions and negotiations accompanying the process of publication and universalization. Epistemological rules are nothing other than the social rules and regularities inscribed in structures and / or in habitus, particularly as regards the way of conducting a discussion (the rules of argumentation) and settling a conflict. Researchers put an end to their experimentation when they think that their experiment is consistent with the norms of their science and can confront the expected criticisms. [It can be seen that scientific discourse is subject to the general law of the production of discourse, a production which is always oriented by the anticipation (unconscious anticipation, on the basis of dispositions) of the positive or negative profits offered by a certain market, with each speaker confronting a certain state of the market, that is, of the social censorship that he anticipates (Bourdieu 1991a, 2001b).] Scientific knowledge is what has survived objections and can withstand future objections. Validated opinion is the opinion that is recognized, negatively at least, because it no longer arouses pertinent objections or because there is no better explanation. In these struggles which accept as their arbiter the verdict of experience, that is to say, what researchers agree to consider as the real, truth is the set of representations regarded as true because they are produced according to the rules defining the production of truth; it is what is agreed on by competitors who agree on the principles of verification, on common methods for the validation of hypotheses.

In a universe such as that of science, individual constructions, which are always in fact collective constructions, are engaged in transactions regulated not by the transcendent rules of epistemology, of a methodology or even of logic, but by the specific principles of sociability imposed by membership of a field which are such that to ignore them or transgress them is to exclude oneself from the field. I am thinking here of a description of the violent, sometimes murderous, treatment to which the author of a seminar presentation may be subjected, which is perfectly legitimate, even irreproachable, so long as it is delivered with formal unimpeachability by those possessing mastery of the implicit rules tacitly accepted by all who enter the game (Tompkins 1988).

The tacit entry conditions associated with the ordinary *illusio* that defines membership of the scientific field imply acceptance of the state of the norms regarding the validation of a scientific fact, and, more precisely, recognition of the very principle of dialectical reason: the fact of playing the game of discussion, dialogue (in the Socratic sense), of subjecting one's experiments and calculations to critical examination, of committing oneself to answering for one's thinking to others, and in a responsible way, that is to say, self-consistently, without contradiction, in short, in compliance with the practical principles of an ethos of argumentation. Knowledge is based not on the subjective self-evidence of an isolated individual but on collective experience, regulated by norms of communication and argumentation.

It follows that the Bachelardian vision of scientific work, which I summed up in the formula 'the scientific fact is won, constructed, observed', has to be expanded and completed. It is tacitly thought that the construction has to be validated by experiment, in a relationship between the experimenter and his object. In fact, the process of knowledge validation as *legitimation* (securing the monopoly of legitimate scientific opinion) concerns the relationship between the subject and the object, but also the relationship between subjects regarding the object (I shall return to this). The fact is won, constructed, observed, in and through the dialectical communication among subjects, that is to say through the process of verification, collective production of truth, in and through negotiation, transaction, and also homologation, ratification by the explicitly expressed consensus – *homologein* – (and not only in the dialectic between hypothesis and experiment). A fact truly becomes a scientific fact only if it is recognized. The construction is socially determined in a twofold way: on the one hand, by the position of the laboratory or scientist within the field; on the other hand, by the categories of perception associated with the position of the receiver (with the effect of imposition, authority, being that much greater the lower this position is in relative terms).

The scientific fact is completely realized as such only when it is constituted by the totality of the field and when everyone has collaborated in constituting it as a known and recognized fact. For example, the receivers of a discovery collaborate in verifying it by trying (unsuccessfully) to destroy it, to refute it. 'Observed' means collectively validated in a process of communication leading to universal recognition (within the limits of the field, that is to say the universe of competent judges). A true idea has an intrinsic force within the scientific universe, in certain social conditions. It is a 'force of conviction' which prevails over the competing rival who tries to refute it and who is forced to lay down his arms. The opponents collaborate in the work of verification through the work they do to criticize, correct and refute.

How do researchers who are competing for the monopoly of truth manage to *homologein*, to say the same thing? [Parenthesis: the social sciences, and especially sociology, have difficulty in realizing this ambition of monopoly, although it is inscribed in the fact that 'the truth is one', because, in the name of, among other things, a contamination of the scientific order by principles of the political order and of democracy, people like to think that truth is 'plural', as the current phrase goes, and that different powers, particularly with symbolic, political, religious and above all journalistic dimensions, are socially armed to claim, with some chance of success, the right to utter the truth about the social world.] The *homologein*, rational agreement, is the product of dialogue, discussion; not just any dialogue, but a dialogue subject to the rules of dialectic (I pointed out in *Pascalian Meditations* (1999a) – in a brief summary of a study I made, many years ago, with Jean Bollack, of the transition from analogical reason to logical reason in ancient Greece – that the gradual development of dialectic and regulated dialogue accompanied the emergence of a philosophical field which saw the gradual construction of the regulation of rule-

governed thought in and through which adversaries learned to
agree on the areas of disagreement and on the means of settling
differences).

The work of verification and the *homologein* which ratifies and
consecrates it presuppose the agreement of the observers on the
principle of homologation. Jacques Merleau-Ponty describes the
emergence, in the sciences of the nineteenth and twentieth centuries,
of a 'community that defines itself by the operations which
enable everyone to attune himself to everyone else' (1965: 184). The
invariant is no longer defined by the immutable, but by its 'identity for
a whole class of observers'. The definition of objectivity which results
from it is no longer based on the operation of an isolated individual
who listens to nature, but brings into play 'the idea of identity
for a class of observers and communicability in an intersubjective
community'. Objectivity depends on the 'the agreement of a class
of observers about what is recorded by the measuring devices in a
very precise experimental situation'. So one can say that there
is no objective reality independent of the conditions of its observation,
without calling into question the fact that what manifests
itself, once these conditions are determined, retains a character of
objectivity.

One might also mention in this respect the analyses by Jean-Claude
Passeron showing the particular ways in which theoretical language is
articulated with empirical protocols (forthcoming: 106–7); or Ian
Hacking's idea that there is a correspondence between a theory and
the instruments it uses: 'We create apparatus that generates data that
confirm theories; we judge the apparatus by its ability to produce data
that fit.' Incommensurability results from the fact that 'phenomena
are produced by fundamentally different techniques, and different
theories answer to different phenomena that are only loosely con-
nected' (Hacking 1992: 54, 57).

It can be seen that, though they have had the merit of emphasizing
the contribution that the process of circulation, neglected by traditional epistemology, makes to the construction of the scientific fact,
laboratory studies have forgotten or greatly underestimated the inseparably social and intellectual logic of that circulation and the effects
of logical and empirical control, and consequently *universalization*,
that it produces. Critical circulation is a process of departiculariza-
tion, of making public, in the twofold sense of officialization and
universalization, leading to what Eugene Garfield (1975) calls the
'obliteration' of the source of an idea, method or discovery 'if it has
already been absorbed into the body of scientific knowledge'. (The

greatest consecration a researcher can receive is to be able to call himself the author of concepts, effects, etc., that have become an-onymous, subjectless.) One might also mention here the admirable analysis by Gerald Holton (1978) showing how Robert Millikan won 'assent' for his work on oil drops because he took care to publish his private experiments. It is also this context which gives their full significance to studies aiming to understand the complex transition from the 'privacy' of the laboratory to the 'publicity' of the field, such as those of Owen Hannaway (1988) or Stephen Shapin (1988). The epistemologists ignore this transition and the transmutation to which it gives rise, but sociologists who identify making-public with publi-city are no better placed to grasp its *inseparably epistemological and social* logic, the very logic which defines the socio-logical process of veri-fication.

[While it is desirable to take note of the role of 'publication', in the sense of making public, becoming public (*Öffentlichkeit*), it is not a form of publicity or public relations, as some advocates of the new sociology of science seem to think – no doubt in good faith, since they try to apply their idea of success in the service of the success of their ideas and act in accordance with their image of scientists, whom they see in their own image ... Putting into practice their vision of the scientific world, they seek to create networks in which the recog-nition of their importance is constituted: social truth comes from the trial of strength, and so one has to be in a position of strength, in journals, publishing houses, etc., in order to have the last word over one's adversaries.]

But there is another way of perverting the logic of officialization-universalization, made possible by the fact that one can mimic, ape, the appearances of universality. In my book on Heidegger, *The Polit-ical Ontology of Martin Heidegger* (1991b), I tried to describe the process whereby one can give the appearances of systematicity and necessity to a vocabulary, which then presents itself as independent of the historical agent who produces it and the social conditions of which it is the product. I could cite countless examples, from sociological and especially economic literature, of this kind of social effort of neutral-ization, which, by mimicking the neutralization effect of the natural sciences, can produce perfectly deceptive 'science effects'. I wish I had the time here to read out and comment on a long letter on economics by Wassily Leontief, entitled 'Academic economics' (1982), in which he shows that this discipline bases its scientific authority on an authoritar-ian collective organization aimed at maintaining collective belief and discipline among 'younger faculty members'.

The process of depersonalization, universalization, departiculariza-tion of which the scientific fact is the product is all the more likely actually to take place the more autonomous and international the field is (of all specialized fields, the scientific field is no doubt the one least enclosed in national boundaries and in which the relative weight of 'compatriots' is least important: the degree of internationalization, which can be measured by various indicators, such as the language used, the places of publication, national or external, etc., is one good index of the degree of autonomy). I will cite here Ben-David: 'The allocation of scientific recognition is usually a supranational and, at least to some extent, supradisciplinary process; the effect of any particular bias is thus minimized' (1991: 341). Because, as I have said, temporal capital is more linked to national fora, to the temporally dominant institutions, such as academies, and dependent on the temporal authorities, whether economic or political, the process of universalization will almost necessarily take the form of an internationalization equivalent to denationalization.

The international dimension is indeed a recourse against the national temporal powers, especially in situations of weak autonomy. Again I will quote Ben-David: 'The individual scientist who happened to be rejected by a disciplinary authority had several courts of appeal. He could submit his paper to several journals, present it as a book to the general scientific community, as Darwin did, or demonstrate it by impressive, highly visible experiments, as did Pasteur and Koch. These appeals were all made to organizations and publics which were separate from organization of teaching and research and were often interdisciplinary in scope and international in their membership' (1991: 338).

What are the strictly epistemological consequences of these analyses? Struggles for the monopoly of the scientifically legitimate representation owe their specificity (one should say their exceptionality) to the fact that, in contrast particularly to what is observed in the artistic field, the logic of competition leads (or forces) scientists to apply at every moment all the available cognitive instruments and all the means of verification that have been accumulated in the course of the whole history of science, and so to give its full efficacy to the arbitrating power of 'reality' (as constructed and structured in accordance with socially defined principles).

The shift from the relationship between a subject (the scientist) and an object to a relationship among subjects (the whole set of agents engaged in the field) regarding the relationship between the subject (the scientist) and his object leads one to reject both the naïve realist vision in which scientific discourse is a direct reflection of reality, a pure recording, and the relativist-constructivist vision, in which scientific discourse is the product of a construction, oriented by interests and cognitive structures, which produces multiple visions of the world, underdetermined by that world. [It may be noted in passing that relativism is based on a realism, for example the observation that there are various and variable interpretations of an unchanged reality; or that what scientists say differs from what they do in reality.] Science is *a construction which brings out a discovery* irreducible to the construction and to the social conditions that made it possible.

Just as one has to move beyond the unacceptable choice between idealist constructivism and realist positivism, towards a *realist rationalism* which argues that scientific construction is the precondition of access to the advent of the 'real' that is called discovery, so one has to move beyond the opposition between the naïvely idealized vision of the 'scientific' community as the enchanted kingdom of the ends of reason and the cynical vision which reduces exchanges between scientists to the calculated brutality of political power relations. The pessimistic vision of science sees only half the truth: it forgets that, in science as in ordinary existence, the officialization strategies through which one puts oneself 'on the right side of the rule' are as much part of reality as are transgressions of the official rule, and that they contribute to the perpetuation and affirmation of the rule and belief in the rule without which there is no longer either regularity or a minimum, external, formal conformity to the rule.

The ruse of scientific reason consists in making necessity out of contingency and chance, and in making a scientific virtue of social necessity. The official vision of science is a collective hypocrisy capable of guaranteeing the minimum of common belief that is necessary for the functioning of a social order; the other face of science is both universally known to all those who take part in the game and unanimously disguised, as a jealously guarded 'open secret' (economists would call it 'common knowledge'). Everyone knows the truth about scientific practices, which the new sociologists of science noisily discover and unveil, and everyone keeps pretending not to know and to believe that things do not happen that way. And if the homage that vice pays to virtue is so unanimous, so unquestioned, so powerfully affirmed in all strategies of universalization, this is because the essential thing, even when one is forced to transgress the rule, is to avoid denouncing the rule that is one of the foundations of the belief (*illusio*) of the group by ratifying practices, albeit common ones, that transgress it and contradict it. Science works, to a large extent, because people manage to believe and make others believe that it works as it is said to work, especially in books of epistemology, and because this collectively maintained collective fiction continues to constitute the ideal norm of practices.

We can now return to the question I raised at the beginning, that of the relationship between truth and history, which is at the heart of the long struggle between philosophy and the social sciences. And we must start, as I have so often said, by rejecting both sides of what is commonly seen as an obligatory choice, on the one hand the logicist absolutism which claims to provide a priori logical foundations for scientific knowledge, and on the other hand historicist relativism. But I must first sketch the general line of the approach I want to follow. First, in place of Kant's universal conditions and a prioris I put socially constituted conditions and a prioris, as Durkheim did for religion and the religious principles of classification and construction of the world in *The Elementary Forms of the Religious Life* and his article on 'The primitive forms of classification'. In a second stage, I would like to show how the process of historicization of Kantian questioning has to lead to a scientific objectivation of the subject of objectivation, a sociology of the knowing subject in its generality and its particularity, in short, to what I call an undertaking of reflexivity, aimed at objectivating the transcendental unconscious that the knowing subject unknowingly invests in acts of knowledge or, to put it another way, his habitus as a historical transcendental – which can be said to be a priori inasmuch as it is a structuring structure which organizes the perception and appreciation of all experience, and a posteriori inasmuch as it is a structured structure produced by a whole series of common or individual learning processes.

There is a danger that, as generally happens, the contribution of sociology will coexist on a parallel plane – but a socially and intellectually lower one (the hierarchy of disciplines is also present in people's minds) – with a dominant tradition of reflexion that remains practically untouched and unchanged. To counter that risk, I will point out that, in a Kantian perspective, objectivity is intersubjectivity, an intersubjective validation, and is therefore opposed to any form of realism aimed at grounding truth in the 'adequation of the mind to the thing'; but Kant does not describe the empirical procedures through which people arrive at that intersubjective agreement – which is acknowledged or (in the name of the separation between the transcendental and the empirical) declared a priori to be based on the agreement of transcendental consciousnesses which, having the same cognitive structures, are universally attuned to the same universal. Objectivity, truth, knowledge do not refer to a relationship between the human mind and a reality independent of the mind. Insisting that we do not have access to 'things in themselves', Kant rejects any realist interpretation. But he does not intend to offer thereby an explanation of natural science considered as an empirical phenomenon; on the contrary, he distinguishes between the 'transcendental' task of philosophy, which is to set out the necessary conditions of truly scientific knowledge, the spatio-temporal structure which makes phenomena possible, and the 'empirical' task of the various sciences.

It is however in a Kantian perspective – but one totally excluded by Kant, in the name of the break between the transcendental and the empirical – that I have placed myself, by taking as my object the search for the *socio-transcendental conditions of knowledge*, that is to say, for the social or socio-cognitive (and not only cognitive) structure, empirically observable (the field etc.), which makes possible phenomena as apprehended by the various sciences or, more precisely, the construction of the scientific object and the scientific fact.

The logical positivists continue to posit that scientific objectivity is only possible by virtue of an a priori mathematical construction which has to be imposed on nature in order for an empirical science of nature to be possible. But this underlying mathematical structure is not, as Kant would have it, the expression of eternal and universal laws of thought. These a priori constructions have to be described as languages. And here it is useful to cite Henri Poincaré, who, reflecting on non-Euclidian geometries, stresses that these constructions have to be described as 'free conventions'. [Poincaré calls 'conventions' those principles of the sciences that are neither self-evidences, nor experimental generalizations, nor hypotheses conjectured with a view to being validated. 'Mathematical axioms are neither a priori synthetic judgements nor experimental facts. They are conventions. Our choice, among all the possible conventions, is guided by experimental facts; but it remains free and is limited only by the necessity of avoiding any contradiction' (Poincaré 1968: part 2, ch. 3). Euclidean geometry is not the most true, but the most convenient (1968: part 2, ch. 4). He also stresses that these conventions are not 'arbitrary', but have 'an experimental origin'.] In fact, Poincaré lets the sociological wolf into the mathematical sheepfold, and into the always somewhat pastoral vision it encourages, when he uses the word 'convention', a term whose social implications he does not at all spell out but which calls into question the idea of universal validity and invites one to consider the social conditions of this conventional validity.

Poincaré is very close to Rudolf Carnap, who, in 1934, posited that there is no notion of universal validity independent of the particular and varied rules of formally specifiable calculations, which are equally possible and legitimate. The notions of 'rationality' or objectivity are 'relative' to the choice of this or that language or linguistic framework. The particular linguistic rules of a given linguistic frame-work define what is correct. The choice among different frameworks can only be the effect of a free convention governed by pragmatic and not rational criteria. Hence the principle of tolerance. In an article entitled 'Empiricism, semantics and ontology' (1950), Carnap distin-guishes internal questions and external questions: internal questions are raised within a linguistic framework and can be answered within the logical rules of this already chosen and accepted linguistic frame-work, in relation to which the notions of objectivity, rationality, validity and truth have meaning; external questions concern choices between different linguistic frameworks, and these choices depend on purely pragmatic criteria of appropriateness for a particular purpose.

Carnap's distinction is entirely analogous to Kuhn's distinction between normal and revolutionary science: the 'puzzle-solving' activ-ities of normal science take place against the background of a gener-ally accepted paradigm which in a relatively undisputed way defines what can count as a correct or incorrect solution. In revolutionary situations, however, the background framework which alone can define 'correctness' is itself in question. This is when one is confronted with the choice between competing paradigms and the transcendent criteria of rationality are absent; and the emergence of a new consen-sus can only be explained by non-rational factors.

Thus the questioning of the universal criteria of rationality was already prefigured in the philosophical tradition that evolved from a 'transcendental' universalism of a Kantian type towards an already relativized notion of rationality as put forward by Carnap. Kuhn merely returns to the Kantian tradition of the a priori, but taken in a relativized, historicized, or, more precisely, sociologized way, as it is by Durkheim, who can be credited with the notion of *socio-transcendental conditions*. Philosophy, closely intertwined with science, has evolved towards a relativized, conventionalist conception of rationality, close to the soci-ology of science, but not taking account of the social factors responsible for the consensual acceptance of Carnap's linguistic framework or Kuhn's paradigm.

It is here that one can address the question of the sociological reading of Wittgenstein, who, as we have seen, has occupied a very important place at the intersection of philosophy and the sociology of science since David Bloor invoked him in order to ground a theory of science in which rationality, objectivity and truth are local socio-cultural norms, conventions adopted and imposed by particular groups: the concepts of 'language game' and 'form of life' which play a central role in the *Philosophical Investigations* are interpreted as referring to sociolinguistic activities associated with particular socio-cultural groups in which practices are regulated by norms conventionally adopted by the groups concerned (Bloor 1983).

Against Bloor's reading, it has been pointed out that Wittgenstein endeavours to deal only with imaginary examples and that he conceives the philosophy he proposes as fundamentally non-empirical: as he constantly points out, 'we are not doing natural science; nor yet natural history – since we can also invent fictitious natural history for our purposes' (Wittgenstein 1953: 230). It is argued that he is only describing the multiple uses of language in our single linguistic community (and not in competing socio-cognitive communities).

With *Philosophical Investigations*, a kind of transcendental logic of a Kantian type aimed at describing the absolutely necessary presuppositions or conditions of possibility of any thought about the real (Friedman 1996), Wittgenstein abandons the logical absolutism of the *Tractatus* for a kind of linguistic pluralism: there are not only several logico-mathematical frameworks, as in Carnap, but several languages for constructing the world. But commentators on Wittgenstein are right to point out that while he refuses all ultimate justifications and foundations and insists that it is we who give meaning and force to logico-mathematical laws through the ways in which we apply them, he does not go so far as to ground the necessity of these laws in agreement and convention. They are 'laws of thought' that express the essence of the human mind and which, as such, should be the object of a non-empirical or, as Wittgenstein puts it, 'grammatical' investigation.

But rather than choose between a 'sociological' reading (in the style of Bloor) and a 'grammatical' reading of Wittgenstein, I want to show that one can maintain the normativity of the 'grammatical' principles without which there is no possible thought while recognizing the historical and social character of all human thought; that it is possible to posit the radical historicity of logical norms and to save reason – without transcendental sleight of hand and without exempting sociological reason itself from the questioning to which sociology subjects all thought.

[Parenthetically, I would like to say that the reference to the two possible readings of Wittgenstein has the virtue of posing very clearly the question of the relationship between logical constraint and social constraint, through the question of universes of practices, 'forms of life', in which logical constraints present themselves in the form of social constraints, such as the world of mathematics or, more broadly, of science. And, noting that all the examples of 'language games' that Wittgenstein gives are taken from societies like our own, I could take the Wittgensteinian break with logicism to its limit and attempt to sketch a solution, Wittgensteinian in inspiration, to the question of the historicity of reason and of the relationship between logical and social constraints. To do this one would only have to see in what I call fields empirical realizations of the 'forms of life' in which different 'language games' are played; and to observe that, among these fields, there are some which, like the scientific field, favour or impose exchanges in which logical constraints take the form of social constraints. They do so because these constraints are in-scribed in the institutionalized procedures regulating entry into the game, in the constraints bearing on exchanges in which the producers have as their clients only the most competent and most critical of their competitors, and above all in the dispositions of the agents, which are partly the product of the mechanisms of the field and of the 'disciplining' they exert.]

It is possible to save reason without invoking, as a deus ex machina, some form or other of the affirmation of the transcendental character of reason. This can be done by describing the gradual emergence of universes in which, in order to be 'right' [*avoir raison*], one has to put forward reasons, demonstrations recognized as consistent, and in which the logic of power relations and struggles of interests is regulated in such a way that the 'force of the best argument' (as Habermas puts it) has a reasonable chance of winning. Scientific fields are universes within which the symbolic power struggles and the struggles of interests that they favour help to give its force to the best argument (and within which Habermas's theory is true, except that it does not raise the question of the social conditions of possibil-ity of these universes and that it inscribes this possibility in universal properties of language through a spuriously historicized form of Kantianism).

So there are universes in which a social consensus is set up regarding truth but which are subject to social constraints favouring rational exchange and obeying *mechanisms of universalization* such as cross-controls; in which the empirical laws of functioning that govern interactions imply the implementation of logical controls; in which symbolic power relations take a quite exceptional form such that, for once, there is an intrinsic force of the true idea, which can draw strength from the logic of competition; in which the ordinary antinomies between interest and reason, force and truth, etc., tend to be weakened or to disappear. And I will quote at this point Popper, who, no doubt with a different intention and in a different logic, argues, like Polanyi, that it is the social nature of science that is responsible for its objectivity: 'Ironically enough, objectivity is closely bound up with the *social aspect of scientific method*, with the fact that science and scientific objectivity do not (and cannot) result from the attempts of an individual scientist to be "objective", but from the friendly-hostile cooperation of many. Scientific objectivity can be described as the inter-subjectivity of scientific method' (Popper 1945: vol. 2, 217).

We have thus reintroduced into Kantian intersubjectivity the social conditions which underlie it and which give it its specifically scientific efficacy. Objectivity is an intersubjective product of the scientific field: grounded in the presuppositions shared within this field, it is the result of the intersubjective agreement within the field. Each field (discipline) is the site of a specific legality (a *nomos*), a product of history, which is embodied in the objective regularities of the functioning of the field and, more precisely, in the mechanisms governing the circulation of information, in the logic of the allocation of rewards, etc., and in the scientific habitus produced by the field, which are the condition of the functioning of the field. Epistemological rules are the conventions established for settling controversies: they govern the confrontation of the scientist with the external world, that is, between theory and experiment, but also with other scientists, enabling him to anticipate criticism and refute it. A good scientist is someone who has a sense of the scientific game, who can anticipate criticism and adapt in advance to the criteria defining acceptable arguments, thus advancing the process of recognition and legitimation; who stops experimenting when he thinks that the experimentation conforms to the socially defined norms of his science and when he feels sufficiently assured to confront his peers. Scientific knowledge is the set of propositions that have survived objections.

What are called epistemic criteria are the formalization of the 'rules of the game' that have to be observed in the field, that is, of the sociological rules of interactions within the field, in particular, rules of argumentation or norms of communication. Argumentation is a collective process performed before an audience and subject to rules. No one is less isolated, less abandoned to himself and his singular originality than a scientist; not only because he always works with others, in laboratories, but because he has taken on all the past and present science of all other scientists, from whom he borrows and to whom he delegates on a permanent basis, and because he is inhabited by a kind of collective super-ego, inscribed in institutions which constantly reassert the rules, and placed in a peer group that is both very critical – the group for whom one writes, and the most daunting of audiences – and very reassuring – the group that underwrites and backs up (with references) and provides guarantees of the quality of the products.

The work of departicularization, universalization, that goes on in the field, through the regulated confrontation of the competitors most inclined and most able to expose as the contingent particularity of a singular opinion any judgement aspiring to validation and, through this, to universal validity, is the reason why the truth recognized by the scientific field is irreducible to its historical and social conditions of production. A truth that has undergone the test of discussion in a field where antagonistic interests, and even opposing power strategies, have battled over it is in no way undermined by the fact that those who discovered it had an interest in discovering it. It even has to be acknowledged that passions, often the most selfish ones, are the motor of this machine, which transforms and transmutes them through a confrontation arbitrated by reference to the constructed real. If truth presents itself as transcendent with respect to the consciousnesses which apprehend it and accept it as such, with respect to the historical subjects who know it and recognize it, this is because it is the product of a collective validation performed in the quite singular conditions of the scientific field, that is to say, in and through the conflictual but regulated cooperation that competition imposes there, and which is capable of enforcing a supersession of antagonistic interests and even the obliteration of all the marks linked to the particular conditions of its emergence. That is what is meant, it seems to me, when people say that physicists working in the quantum domain have no doubts about the objectivity of the knowledge they give of it, because their experiments are reproducible by researchers armed with the competence needed in order to invalidate them.

III

Why the social sciences must take themselves as their object

In raising the problem of knowledge in the way that I have, I have constantly been thinking of the social sciences, of which I have in the past denied the particularity. I did so not out of some kind of positivistic scientism, as some may think or pretend to think, but because exaltation of the 'difference' of the social sciences is often no more than a way of decreeing the impossibility of a scientific understanding of their object. I am thinking for example of a book by Adolf Grünbaum (1984) which describes the attempts by some philosophers, Habermas, Ricoeur, etc., to set a priori limits to these sciences. (And this I find absolutely unjustifiable: why postulate that certain things are unknowable, and, moreover, do so a priori, before any experience? Those who are hostile to science have displaced and concentrated their fury onto the social sciences and, more precisely, onto sociology – no doubt thereby helping to slow down its development – perhaps because the natural sciences no longer offer them any scope for attack. They decree unknowable a certain number of things, such as the religious and all its substitutes, art, and science, which one should cease to try to explain.) It was against this multiform resistance to the social sciences that *The Craft of Sociology* (Bourdieu, Chamboredon and Passeron 1991) insisted that the social sciences are sciences like others, except that they encounter particular difficulty in being sciences like others.

That difficulty appears perhaps even more clearly to me now, and it seems to me that, in order to carry out the scientific project in the social sciences, a further step is needed, one which the natural sciences do not require. To bring to light what is 'the hidden' par excellence, what escapes the gaze of science because it is hidden in the very gaze of the scientist, the transcendental unconscious, one has to historicize the subject of historicization, to objectivate the subject of the objectivation, that is, the *historical transcendental*, the objectivation of which is the precondition for the access of science to self-awareness, in other words, to knowledge of its historical presuppositions. The instrument of objectivation constituted by the social sciences has to be asked to provide the means of rescuing these sciences from the relativization to which they are exposed so long as their productions remain determined by the unconscious determinations that are inscribed in the scientist's mind or in the social conditions within which he produces. And to do this, they have to confront the relativistic or sceptical circle and break it by implementing – in order to perform the science of the social sciences and of the scientists who produce them – all the instruments that these very sciences provide and so produce the means of countering the social determinations to which those sciences are exposed.

To understand one of the major principles of the particularity of the social sciences, one only has to examine a criterion that I have already referred to when raising the question of the relationship between scientificity and autonomy. The various sciences could be distributed according to the degree of autonomy of the field of scientific production with respect to the various forms of external pressure – economic, political, etc. In fields with weak autonomy, which are therefore deeply immersed in social relations, such as astronomy or physics in their initial phase, the great founding revolutions were also religious revolutions which could be resisted politically, with some chance of success (in least in the short term), and which, like those of Copernicus or Galileo, utterly transformed the worldview in all its dimensions. By contrast, the more autonomous a science is, the more, as Bachelard observed, it tends to be nothing less than the site of a permanent revolution, but one which is increasingly devoid of political or religious implications. In a very autonomous field, it is the field that defines not only the ordinary order of 'normal science', but also the extra-ordinary breaks, 'orderly revolutions' as Bachelard calls them.

One may wonder why the social sciences have so much difficulty in winning recognition of their autonomy, why it is so hard to gain acceptance for a discovery outside the field and even within it. The social sciences, and especially sociology, have an object too important (it interests everyone, starting with the powerful), too controversial, for it to be left to their discretion, abandoned to their law alone, too important and too controversial in terms of social life, the social order and the symbolic order, for them to be granted the same degree of autonomy as is given to the other sciences and for them to be allowed the monopoly of the production of truth. And, indeed, everyone feels entitled to have their say in sociology and to enter into the struggle over the legitimate view of the social world, in which the sociologist also intervenes, but with a quite special ambition, which is granted unproblematically to other scientists but which in his case tends to be seen as monstrous: to utter the truth or, worse, to define the conditions in which one can utter the truth.

So social science is particularly exposed to heteronomy, because external pressure is particularly strong there and because the internal conditions for autonomy (in particular the requirement of a 'ticket of entry') are very difficult to set up. Another reason for the weak autonomy of the fields of the social sciences is that, within these fields themselves, agents with unequal degrees of autonomy confront one another and, as in the least autonomous fields, the most heteronomous researchers and their 'endoxic' truths, as Aristotle put it, have, by definition, more chance of winning social recognition against autonomous researchers: those who are scientifically most dominated are those most inclined to submit to external demands, whether from the right or from the left (this is what I call the law of Zhdanovism), and better prepared, often by default, to satisfy those demands and therefore more likely to win the day in the logic of the plebiscite – or of 'audience ratings'. Considerable freedom is allowed, within the field itself, to those who contradict the very *nomos* of the field and who are protected against the symbolic sanctions which, in other fields, strike those who fall short of the fundamental principles of the field. Propositions that are incoherent or incompatible with the facts are more likely to perpetuate themselves and even to thrive than in the most autonomous scientific fields, so long as, both inside and outside the field, they carry sufficient social weight to compensate for their scientific inadequacy or insignificance, in particular by providing them with material and institutional support (grants, subsidies, posts, etc.). By the same token, everything that defines a highly autonomous field and is linked to the self-enclosure of the subfield of restricted production, such as mechanisms of cross-control, has difficulty in becoming established.

Together with its weak entry conditions leading to low cross-control and its very high social stakes, social science has a third particularity making it especially difficult to make the social break that is the precondition of scientific construction. We have seen that the scientific struggle is arbitrated by reference to the constructed 'real'. In the social sciences, the 'real' is indeed external to and independent of knowledge, but it is itself a social construction, a product of past struggles which, at least in this respect, remains at stake in present struggles. (This becomes clear, even in the case of history, as soon as one tackles events which are still issues at stake for contemporaries.) So a constructivist vision of science has to be combined with a constructivist vision of the scientific object: social facts are socially constructed, and every social agent, like the scientist, more or less successfully constructs, and seeks to impose, with more or less strength, his individual vision of reality, his 'point of view'. That is why sociology, whether it wants to or not (and mostly it does), is an actor in the struggles it describes.

Social science is, then, a social construction of a social construction. There is in the object itself – in social reality as a whole and in the social microcosm within which the scientific representation of that reality is constructed, the scientific field – a struggle over (for) the construction of the object, in which social science participates in a twofold way: caught up in the game, it undergoes its constraints and produces some (no doubt limited) effects within it. The analyst is part of the world that he is trying to objectivate and the science he produces is only one of the forces that confront one another within that world. Scientific truth does not impose itself by itself, by the sheer force of its argumentative reason (not even in the scientific field). Sociology is socially weak, and all the weaker, no doubt, the more scientific it is. Social agents, especially when they occupy dominant positions, are not only ignorant, they do not want to know (for example, scientific analysis of television gives an opportunity to observe a direct confrontation between the holders of temporal power over that universe and the science that shows the truth). Sociology cannot hope for the unanimous recognition enjoyed by the natural sciences (whose object is no longer at all – or only very little – at stake in social struggles outside the field) and it is condemned to be contested, 'controversial'.

1   Objectivating the subject of objectivation

Reflexivity is not only the only way out of the contradiction which consists in demanding a relativizing critique and relativism for the other sciences, while remaining attached to a realist epistemology.

Understood as the effort whereby social science, taking itself for its object, uses its own weapons to understand and check itself, it is a particularly effective means of increasing the chances of attaining truth by increasing the cross-controls and providing the principles of a technical critique, which makes it possible to keep closer watch over the factors capable of biasing research. It is not a matter of pursuing a new form of absolute knowledge, but of exercising a specific form of epistemological vigilance, the very form that this vigilance must take in an area where the epistemological obstacles are first and foremost social obstacles.

The science most sensitive to social determinisms must indeed find within itself the resources which, methodically applied as a critical device (and disposition), can enable it to limit the effects of historical and social determinisms. To be able to apply to their own practice the objectivating techniques that they apply to the other sciences, sociologists have to convert reflexivity into a disposition constitutive of their scientific habitus, a *reflexivity reflex*, capable of acting not *ex post*, on the *opus operatum*, but *a priori*, on the *modus operandi* (a disposition that will make it impossible, for example, to analyse the apparent differences in statistical data from different countries without looking for the differences hidden between the categories of analysis or the conditions of data gathering linked to the different national traditions which may be responsible for these differences or their absence).

But sociologists must first avoid the temptation of indulging in the type of reflexivity that could be called *narcissistic*, not only because it is very often limited to a complacent looking-back by the researcher on his own experience, but also because it is its own end and leads to no practical effect. In spite of the contributions it can by itself make to a better knowledge of scientific practice, I would readily place in this category reflexivity as practised by the ethnomethodologists, which owes its special seductiveness to the air of radicality it gives itself by presenting itself as a penetrating critique of established forms of social science. To try to identify the logic of the various 'coding games', Garfinkel and Sachs (1986) observed two students who had been asked to code the files of psychiatric hospital patients in accordance with standardized instructions. They enumerate the 'ad hoc considerations' that the coders adopted in order to fit the content of the files to the coding schedule, in particular, rhetorical terms such as 'etc., let it pass, unless', and note that they use their knowledge of the clinic they work in (and more generally of the social world) to make these correspondences. All this leads to the conclusion that scientific work is more constitutive than descriptive or constative (which is a way of calling into question the claim of the social sciences to scientificity).

Observations and reflexions such as those of Garfinkel and Sachs may at least have the effect of shaking the positivistic confidence of ordinary statisticians in their taxonomies and routinized procedures. And it is clear what benefits a realist conception of reflexivity can derive from analyses of this kind, which I have in fact myself carried out on many occasions. But that is on condition that one is guided by an intention that could be called *reformist*, inasmuch as it explicitly undertakes to seek in social science and in the knowledge that it can provide, especially about social science itself, its operations and pre-suppositions, instruments that are indispensable for a reflexive cri-tique capable of giving it a higher degree of freedom with respect to the social constraints and necessities that bear on it as they do on all human activity.

But this practical reflexivity can take on its full force only if the analysis of the implications and presuppositions of the routine oper-ations of scientific practice is taken further into a genuine critique (in Kant's sense) of the social conditions of possibility and the limits of the forms of thought that the scientist ignorant of those conditions unwittingly engages in his research and which, unknown to him, that is to say, in his place, perform the most specifically scientific oper-ations, such as the construction of the object of science. For example, a truly sociological inquiry into coding operations would have to try to objectivate the taxonomies implemented by the coders (students employed to code the data or the authors of the coding grid), which may belong to the common anthropological unconscious, like those I discovered in a public-opinion questionnaire on politicians (analysed in the appendix to *Distinction* (1984)), or to an academic unconscious, such as the 'categories of professorial understanding' (Bourdieu 1975b) that I derived from the judgements formulated by a teacher to justify his marks and classifications; and which, in both cases, can therefore be related to their social conditions of production.

It was in this way that reflexion on the concrete operations of coding, the very ones that I was applying in my own surveys, or those that had been applied by the producers of the statistics that I had to use (in particular, surveys by INSEE, the national statistics institute), led me to relate the categories or classification systems used to the users and originators of these classifications and to the social conditions of their production (in particular their educational training), with the objectivation of this relationship providing an effective means of understanding and allowing for its effects. For example, there is no more perfect manifestation of what I have called 'state thinking' than the categories of state statistics, which reveal their arbitrariness (normally masked by the routine of an authorized institution) only when they are thrown into disarray by an 'unclassifiable' reality – such as the populations that have newly emerged, on the uncertain border between adolescence and adulthood, particularly in association with the prolonging of education and changes in matrimonial customs, and which cannot readily be classified as adolescent or adult, students or wage-earners, married or single, employed or unemployed. But state thinking is so powerful, especially in the heads of the state scientists trained by the grandes écoles of the French state, that the confounding of the classificatory routines and of the compromises that normally make it possible to save them, such as all the equivalents of the American coder's 'let it pass' – assimilations, catch-all categories, construction of indices, etc. – would not have been enough to provoke a questioning of bureaucratic, state-guaranteed taxonomies if our state statisticians had not had the occasion to encounter a reflexive tradition that could only be born and develop at the pole of 'pure', bureaucratically irresponsible science within the social sciences.

To this one should add, to complete the marking of the difference from narcissistic reflexivity, that reformist reflexivity is not something done by one person alone and that it can exert its full effect only if it is incumbent upon all the agents engaged in the field. The sociologically armed epistemological vigilance that each researcher can apply on his own behalf can only be strengthened by the generalizing of the imperative of reflexivity and the spreading of the indispensable instruments for complying with it; this alone can institute reflexivity as the common law of the field, which would thus become characterized by a sociological critique of all by all that would intensify the effects of the epistemological critique of all by all.

This reformist conception of reflexivity can, in each researcher and, a fortiori, on the scale of a collective such as a team or a laboratory, become the principle of a kind of *epistemological prudence* making it possible to anticipate the probable chances of error or, more broadly, the tendencies and temptations inherent in a system of dispositions, in a position or in the relationship between the two. For example, when one has read Charles Soulié's work (1995) on the choice of subjects for philosophy dissertations and theses, one is less likely to be manipulated by the determinisms linked to sex, social origin and educational background which commonly orient such choices; similarly, when one is aware of the tendency of the 'scholarship boy' towards awe-struck hyperidentification with the educational system, one is better prepared to resist the effects of academic thinking. Another example: if, like Weber describing the 'tendencies of the body of priests', one speaks of the tendencies of the professorial corps, one can increase one's chances of escaping the most typical of them, the inclination towards the scholastic bias, the probable destiny of so many readings by *lectores*, and of looking in a quite different way at a genealogy, a typically scholastic construction which, under the appearance of seeming to deliver the truth of kinship, prevents one from grasping the practical experience of the kinship network and of the strategies aimed, for example, at maintaining it. But one can go beyond knowledge of the most common tendencies and endeavour to identify the tendencies characteristic of the body of philosophy teachers or, more precisely, French philosophy teachers, or, still more precisely, French philosophy teachers trained in the 1950s, and so give oneself some chance of anticipating probable destinies and avoiding them. Similarly, the discovery of the link between the epistemological couples described by Bachelard and the dualistic structure of fields inclines one to distrust dualisms and to subject them to a sociological and not only epistemological critique. In short, the socioanalysis of the scientific mind as I have sketched it seems to me to be a principle of freedom, and therefore of intelligence.

An undertaking of objectivation is scientifically controlled only to the extent of the preliminary objectivation that has been applied to the subject of the objectivation. For example, when I undertake to objectivate an object like the French university system in which I am caught up, I have as my aim, and I need to know this, to objectivate a whole area of my specific unconscious that is liable to obstruct knowledge of the object, all progress in knowledge of the object being inseparably progress in knowledge of one's relation to the object, and therefore in mastery of one's unanalysed relation to the object (the 'polemic of scientific reason' that Bachelard refers to almost always presupposes a suspension of polemics in the ordinary sense). In other words, I have that much more chance of being objective the more completely I have objectivated my own (social, academic, etc.) position and interests, in particular the specifically academic ones, linked to that position.

[To give an example of the 'dialectical' relationship between self-analysis and the analysis that is at the heart of the *work of objectivation*, I could relate here the whole history of the survey which led to *Homo Academicus* (1988a) – unfortunately I did not have the 'reflexive reflex' of keeping a research diary, and I would have to work from memory. But, to extend the example of coding, I discovered for example that there were no criteria of scientific quality (except for distinctions like gold, silver or bronze medals, which are too rare to serve as an effective and pertinent coding criterion). I was therefore led to construct indices of scientific recognition and, by the same token, forced to reflect not only on the different treatment I had to give to 'artificial' categories and to categories already constituted in reality (such as sex), but also on the very absence of principles of specific hierarchization in a body literally obsessed by classifications and hierarchies. This led me to invent the idea of a system of collective defence, in which the absence of criteria of 'scientific value' is one element, and which enables individuals, with the complicity of the group, to protect themselves against the probable effects of a rigorous system of measurement of 'scientific value' – probably because such a system would be so painful for most of those who are engaged in scientific life that everyone strives to behave as if this hierarchy were incapable of being evaluated and that, as soon as an instrument of measurement appears, such as the citation index, it can be rejected on various grounds, such as that it favours big laboratories, or English-speaking scientists, etc. In contrast to what happens when one classifies beetles, one is here classifying classifiers who do not accept being classified, who may even dispute the criteria of classification or the very principle of classification, in the name of principles of classification which themselves depend on their positions within the classifications. It can be seen that, by stages, this reflexion on what was initially no more than a technical problem leads one to reflect on the status and function of the sociologist and sociology, and on the general and particular conditions in which one can practise the craft of sociology.]

When one makes the objectivation of the subject of objectivation the necessary precondition for scientific objectivation, one is not only trying to apply the scientific methods of objectivation to scientific practice (as in Garfinkel's example); one is also bringing to light scientifically the social conditions of possibility of construction, that is to say, the social conditions of sociological construction and of the subject of this construction. [It is no accident that the ethnomethodologists forget this second moment, since, although they point out that the social world is constructed, they forget that the constructors are themselves socially constructed and that their construction depends on their position in the objective social space that science has to construct.]

To recapitulate, what has to be objectivated is not the lived experience of the knowing subject, but the social conditions of possibility, and therefore the effects and limits, of this experience and, among other things, of the act of objectivation. What has to be mastered is the subjective relation to the object – which, when it is not taken into account, and when it orients choices of object, method, etc., is one of the most powerful factors of error – and the social conditions of production of this relationship, the social world that produced the specialty and the specialist (anthropologist, sociologist or historian) and the unconscious anthropology that he engages in his scientific practice.

This work of objectivation of the subject of objectivation must be carried out at three levels: one first has to objectify the position of the subject of objectivation in the overall social space, his or her original position and trajectory, his or her membership of and commitment to social and religious groups (this is the most visible factor of distortion, the most commonly perceived and therefore the least dangerous); then one has to objectivate the position he or she occupies within the field of specialists (and the position of this field, this discipline, in the field of the social sciences), each discipline having its own traditions and na- tional particularities, its obligatory problematics, its habits of thought, its shared beliefs and self-evidences, its rituals and consecrations, its constraints as regards publication of findings, its specific forms of censorship, not to mention the whole set of presuppositions inscribed in the collective history of the specialty (the academic unconscious); thirdly, one has to objectivate everything that is linked to membership of the scholastic universe, paying particular attention to the illusion of the absence of illusion, of the pure, absolute, 'disinterested' point of view. The sociology of intellectuals brings to light the particular form of interest which is the interest in disinterestedness (contrary to the illusion of Tawney, Durkheim and Peirce) (Haskell 1984).

2   Sketch for a self-analysis

I have pointed out that reflexive analysis must consider successively position in the social space, position in the field and position in the scholastic universe. How, without surrendering to narcissistic self- indulgence, can one apply this programme to oneself and perform the sociology of oneself, one's self-socioanalysis, given that such an analysis can only be a starting-point and that the sociology of the object that I am, the objectivation of my point of view, is a necessarily collective task?

Paradoxically, the objectivation of the point of view is the surest implementation of the 'principle of charity' (or generosity) and I am likely, in applying it, to seem to be falling into self-indulgence: to understand something is to make it 'necessary', to justify it in existing. Flaubert complained that the social science of his day was incapable of 'taking the point of view of the author', and he was right, if that is taken to mean situating itself where the author situated himself, at the point he occupied within the world and from which he saw the world;

to place oneself at that point is to take the point of view on the world that is his, to understand it as he understood it, and so, in a sense, to justify it.

A point of view is first of all a view taken from a particular point (*Gesichtspunkt*), a particular position in space and, in the sense in which I shall mean it here, in the social space: to objectivate the subject of objectivation, the (objectivating) point of view, is to break with the illusion of the absolute point of view, which is characteristic of every point of view (initially condemned to be unaware that it is only a point of view); it is therefore also a perspective view (*Schau*): all perceptions, visions, beliefs, expectations, hopes, etc., are socially structured and socially conditioned and they obey a law which defines the principle of their variation, the law of the correspondence between positions and position-takings. Individual A's perception is to individual B's perception as A's position is to B's position, with the habitus making the connection between the space of positions and the space of points of view.

But a point of view is also a point in a space (*Standpunkt*), a point of space where one stands in order to take a view, a point of view in the first sense, on that space: to conceive the point of view in this way is to conceive it differentially, relationally, in terms of the possible alternative positions to which it is opposed in different respects (income, qualifications, etc.). And, by the same token, it means constituting as such the space of points of view. This very precisely defines one of the tasks of science, as the objectivation of the space of points of view from a new point of view, which only scientific work, armed with theoretical and technical instruments (such as the geometrical analysis of data), enables one to take – this point of view on all points of view being, according to Leibniz, the point of view of God, the only one capable of producing the 'geometral of all perspectives', the geometric locus of all points of view, in both senses of the term, that is to say, of all positions and all position-takings, which science can only indefinitely approach and which remains, in terms of another geometrical metaphor, borrowed from Kant this time, a *focus imaginarius*, a (provisionally) inaccessible limit.

Let me reassure you that this sketch for a self-socioanalysis will have nothing of the confession about it, and if there are any confessions, they will be only very impersonal ones. In fact, as I have already suggested, all research in the social sciences, when one knows how to use it to that end, is a form of socioanalysis; and this is especially true, of course, of the history and sociology of education and intellectuals (I never tire of quoting Durkheim's 'the unconscious is history'). Now, I can constitute as such my own point of view, and understand it at least partially as it objectively is (in particular as regards its limits) only by constructing and understanding the field within which it defines itself as occupying a certain position, a certain point.

[To give you a less abstract and perhaps also more amusing idea of the reversal that consists in taking a point of view on one's own point of view, in objectivating a person who, like the researcher, objectivates professionally, I will mention a story written by David Garnett, *A Man in the Zoo*. This tells the tale of a young man who quarrels with his girlfriend during a visit to a zoo and, in despair, writes to the director of the zoo to offer him a mammal that is missing from his collection, man. He is put in a cage, alongside the chimpanzee, with a label saying: 'Homo Sapiens. Man. This specimen was presented by John Cromartie, Esq. Visitors are requested not to irritate the Man by personal remarks.']

So, after all these preliminaries, I will aim to do in respect of myself roughly what I did at the start for the various trends in the sociology of science that I referred to; and thereby to define my differential position.

I will begin by indicating the position that I occupied in the field of the social sciences at various moments in my trajectory and perhaps, for the sake of the parallelism with the other currents in the sociology of science, in the subfield of the sociology of science, at the moment when I wrote my first text on the scientific field, in the early 1970s, that is to say, at a time when the 'new sociology of science' had not yet emerged, although the social conditions which no doubt contributed to its success on the campuses were then taking shape.

But I should perhaps first examine the position I occupied in the field at the start, in and around the 1950s, that of the '*normalien* philosophy student', a position of distinction at the summit of the educational system at a time when philosophy could appear triumphant. In fact I have given there the essential part of what is needed in order to explain and understand my subsequent trajectory within the university field, except perhaps the fact that in those days, in those places, sociology, and to a lesser extent anthropology, were minor, even despised disciplines (but for more detail I refer you to the passage in *Pascalian Meditations* entitled 'Impersonal confessions' – 1999a).

Another decisive moment was my entry into the scientific field, in the 1960s. Understanding, in this case, means understanding the field against which and with which one has defined oneself; and also understanding the distance from the field, and its determinisms, that can be given by a certain use of reflexivity: I would need to reread here an article entitled 'Sociology and philosophy in France since 1945: death and resurrection of a philosophy without subject', which I wrote with Jean-Claude Passeron for the American journal *Social Research* (Bourdieu and Passeron 1967). That text, although somewhat inflated with *normalien* pretension and rhetorical padding, said two essential and, I think, profoundly true things about the field of the social sciences: first, that the swing of the pendulum that led the *normaliens* of the 1930s, in particular Sartre and Aron, to react against Durkheimianism, which was perceived as somewhat 'totalitarian', had gone back in the opposite direction by the early 1960s, particularly following the example of Lévi-Strauss and structural anthropology, taking it back to what was then called, on the side of *Esprit* and Paul Ricoeur, a 'philosophy without subject' (it has swung the other way again since the 1980s ...); secondly, that sociology as a discipline was a 'refuge' and was strongly influenced by the dominant model of the scientism imported from America by Lazarsfeld. [The sociology of sociology would have the beneficial effect of freeing the social sciences from such 'swings of the pendulum', which are often described as phenomena of fashion but are in reality largely the effect of the reactive movements of the new entrants, against the positions taken by the dominant figures, who are also the oldest, their elders.]

Constructing the *space of possibles* that presented itself to me as I entered the field means reconstituting the space of the positions constitutive of the field as they could be apprehended from a certain socially constituted point of view, my own, on the field (a point of view that had been set up through the whole social trajectory leading to the position I occupied, and also through that position – that of assistant to Raymond Aron at the Sorbonne and general secretary of the research centre he had recently set up within the École des hautes études). To reconstitute the space of possibles, one has to start by reconstructing the space of the social sciences, in particular the relative positions of the various disciplines or specialties. The space of sociology was already constituted, and Georges Gurvitch's *Traité de sociologie*, which ratified the distribution of sociology among various 'specialties' and 'specialists', gives a good picture of it – a closed world in which all the places were assigned. The older generation held all the dominant positions, which, at that moment, were all professorial teaching (not research) chairs at the Sorbonne (which – to give the scale of the morphological changes that have occurred since then, with the proliferation of posts, especially at junior level – counted a total of just *three* professors of sociology and social psychology, each of whom had just one assistant): Georges Gurvitch, who ruled the Sorbonne in notoriously despotic fashion; Jean Stoetzel, who taught social psychology at the Sorbonne and ran the Centre d'études sociologiques, but also IFOP [the French Institute of Public Opinion], and who controlled the CNRS; and finally Raymond Aron, recently appointed at the Sorbonne, who, to a relational perception (imposed by the functioning as a field), appeared as offering an opening to those who wanted to escape from the forced choice between the theoreticist sociology of Gurvitch and the scientistic, Americanized psychosociology of Stoetzel, who had edited a large, mediocre compilation of American writings on public opinion. The rising generation, all aged around forty, distributed among themselves the research, and also the new powers, linked to the creation of laboratories and journals, in accordance with a division into special-ties, often defined by common-sense concepts, and clearly demarcated as so many fiefdoms: the sociology of work was Alain Touraine, and secondarily Jean-Daniel Reynaud and Jean-René Tréanton; the soci-ology of education was Viviane Isambert; the sociology of religion, François-André Isambert; rural sociology, Henri Mendras; urban soci-ology, Paul-Henri Chombard de Lauwe; the sociology of leisure, Joffre Dumazedier ... with no doubt a few other minor or marginal provinces that I forget. The space was marked out by three or four recently founded major journals: the *Revue française de sociologie*, controlled by Stoetzel and some second-generation researchers (Raymond Boudon inherited it a few years later); the *Cahiers inter-nationaux de sociologie*, controlled by Gurvitch (and inherited by Georges Balandier); the *Archives européennes de sociologie*, founded by Aron, and edited by Éric de Dampierre; and a few secondary journals, less decisive in the structure – rather like Georges Friedman in the older generation – *Sociologie du travail* and *Études rurales*.

One should also mention *L'Homme*, a journal founded and edited by Lévi-Strauss, which, although almost entirely devoted to anthro-pology, exerted a great attraction on a number of new entrants (of whom I was one). By this can be seen the eminent position of anthro-pology, and the dominated position of sociology, within the space of the disciplines. One should even say doubly dominated – within the field of the hard sciences, where it had difficulty in being accepted (if indeed it had any such ambition ... we were a long way from the time of Durkheim), while anthropology, through Lévi-Strauss, was fighting for recognition as a science in its own right (particularly by making use of the reference to linguistics, which was then at its zenith); and also in the field of the literary disciplines, where, for many philosophers, still full of statutory self-assurance, and for many literary scholars concerned for distinction (there still are many today, and even here), the 'human sciences' were jumped-up newcomers and intruders.

Not surprisingly, this 'refuge' discipline – a welcoming, indeed, too welcoming haven that, as Yvette Delsaut has neatly put it, 'did not intimidate' – had only a small stratum of category A staff, made up mainly of professors teaching the history of the discipline and doing little or no research, and a mass (not in fact a very large one) of members of category B, who only very rarely had the *agrégation* (when they did, it was most often in philosophy) and who came from very varied academic origins (the *licence* [equivalent of Bachelor's degree] in sociology did not exist when the second generation entered the field). These researchers, who had not received the single and homogenizing training that would have given them a sense of unity, devoted themselves mainly to empirical research which was for the most part as ill-armed theoretically as it was empirically, distinguished themselves (from the historians for example) by all the indices of an *enormous dispersion* (especially as regards their level of qualifications) which was not conducive to the establishment of a universe of rational discussion. One could speak of a *pariah discipline*: the 'devaluation' that, in an intellectual milieu nonetheless very occupied and preoccupied with politics (but many commitments, especially those in the Communist Party, are still a way, albeit a somewhat paradoxical one, of keeping the social world at a distance), affected everything that had to do with social matters intensified a dominated position within the university field. On this point, although the situation has somewhat evolved, the essence of this description remains true – as is attested by the fact, which countless indices confirm, that the move from philosophy to sociology is accompanied, now as in Durkheim's day, by a kind of 'degradation'; or the fact that, among the 'idées reçues' most deeply implanted in the brains of philosophers or literary scholars, there is the conviction that, whatever the problem, one has to 'go beyond sociology' or 'rise above purely sociological explanation' (in the name of the denial of 'sociologism').

But sociology can also be a means of continuing politics by other means (in this respect, no doubt, it is opposed to psychology, which is strongly feminized in its recruitment) and, in Auguste Comte's classification of the sciences, it appears as the crowning discipline, capable of rivalling philosophy when it comes to understanding the things of the world in their totality. (Raymond Aron, who transported into sociology the total ambitions of Sartrean-style philosophy, wrote a book entitled no less than 'Peace and War among Nations' (*Paix et*

Guerre entre les nations, 1962).) Furthermore, the reference to America, which set it apart from the canonical disciplines of history, literature or philosophy, gave it an air of modernity. In short, it was a strongly dispersed discipline which, both in its social definition and in the population it attracted – teachers, researchers and students – offered an ambiguous, even contradictory image.

One would also need to analyse the relationship between sociology and history, which again is not simple – and, to give a further indication of the pariah status of the sociologist, I would simply point to the care historians take to exclude themselves from the social sciences and, while they readily declare their allegiance to anthropology, to keep their distance from sociology, from which, like the philosophers, they nonetheless borrow a lot, especially as regards conceptual tools. But there too, for more details, I would refer to a discussion I had, a few years ago, with a German historian of the *Annales* school (Bourdieu 1995).

To construct the space of possibles that is generated in the relationship between a habitus and a field, I again need to sketch briefly (I shall return to this) the characteristics of the habitus that I brought into this field. This habitus, because of my social trajectory, was not 'modal' in the philosophical field, and, especially because of my educational trajectory, neither was it modal in the sociological field, and it set me apart from most of my philosopher and sociologist contemporaries. Furthermore, returning from Algeria with experience as an anthropologist which, acquired in the difficult conditions of the war of liberation, had marked for me a decisive break with my previous academic experience, I was led to take a rather lofty view of sociology and sociologists, with the philosopher's view reinforced by that of the anthropologist.

Not surprisingly, in those conditions, the space of possibles that offered itself to could not be reduced to the one presented to me by the positions constituted as sociological, in France or abroad, in other words in the United States and, secondarily, in Germany and Britain. It is certain that everything inclined me to refuse to be confined within sociology, or even within anthropology and philosophy, and to see my work in relation to the whole field of the social sciences and philosophy. [The fact of being here both the subject and the object of the analysis intensifies a very common difficulty in sociological analysis, the danger that the interpretations put forward of practices – what are sometimes called 'objective intentions' – may be understood as express intentions of the acting subject, intentional strategies, explicit projects. When, for example (as one cannot fail to do, as a point of method), I relate my intellectual projects, which were particularly broad, ignoring the frontiers between specialties, but

also between sociology and philosophy, to my move from philosophy, a prestigious discipline, where some of my peers as a student remained (something
which was probably very important subjectively), to sociology, and the loss of
symbolic capital that was 'objectively' entailed, this does not mean that my
choices of object or method were inspired in me, consciously or quasi-cynically,
by the *intention* of safeguarding that capital.]

The fact that I saw myself, initially, as an anthropologist, which
was the subjectively most acceptable way of accepting the loss of
status linked to the move from philosophy to the social sciences, led
me to import into sociology much of what I had learned in doing
philosophy and anthropology: techniques (such as the intensive use of
photography – I had taken many pictures in Algeria), methods (such
as ethnographic observation or conversations with subjects whom I
treated more as informants than as 'respondents') and, perhaps above
all, problems and modes of thought which led me to the methodological polytheism that I subsequently and gradually theorized (such
as the combination of statistical analysis and direct observation of
groups, in the case of *Un Art moyen* (Bourdieu et al. 1990)). This
was, then, a way of moving into sociology, but a *redefined and
ennobled* sociology (traces of all this can be seen in the Prologue to
Travail et Travailleurs en Algérie – Bourdieu et al. 1963 – or in the
preface to *Un Art moyen*), in accordance with the Ben-David and
Collins model discussed earlier.

No doubt it was the same social principles (together with my
training in epistemology) that inspired in me a refusal of (or contempt
for) the scientistic definition of sociology, and in particular my rejection of specialization, which was taken over from the model of the
most advanced sciences but seemed to me quite unjustified in the case
of a science still in its beginnings like sociology (I especially remember
the sense of scandal I felt, in the mid-1960s, at the World Congress of
Sociology in Varna, at the unjustifiable divisions of the discipline into
sociology of education, sociology of culture and sociology of the intellectuals, with each of these sciences being able to abandon the true
explanatory principles of its object to another). And so I quite naturally thought that one needed to work on reunifying an artificially
fragmented social science, without falling into the academic incanta-
tions on the 'total social fact' portentously intoned by some of the
masters of the Sorbonne; and, both in my research and in the publications I promoted in the series Le Sens Commun that I had begun to
edit for Éditions de Minuit, I tried to bring together social history and
sociology, the history of philosophy and the history of art (with
authors like Erwin Panofsky and Michael Baxandall), anthropology,
history, linguistics, and so on. I was thus led into a kind of scientific

practice, converted by stages into a deliberate stance, which could be said, in some ways, to be 'anti-everything' and, in another respect, 'catch-all', as is said of some political parties. And so I found myself – without ever having explicitly wished it and certainly without any 'imperialist' ambition – present in the totality of the field of the social sciences.

What this means is that, even if I may have conceived and explicitly formulated the project, by reference to Durkheim's great model, I never had the explicit intention of bringing about a revolution in the social sciences, except perhaps against the American model, which was then dominant, worldwide, and more especially against the separation that it made, and managed to enforce universally, between 'theory' and 'methodology' (embodied in the opposition between Parsons and Lazarsfeld, who each had their 'local subsidiaries' and 'trading posts' – their editors, translators and commentators in France); and also, but on another terrain, against philosophy, which, in its dominant social definition, seemed to me to represent a major obstacle to the progress of the social sciences (I have often defined myself, in this very place, in somewhat ironic terms, as the leader of a movement for the liberation of the social sciences from the grip of philosophy). I had no more indulgence for sociologists who saw their visit to the USA as a kind of initiatory voyage than I had had, ten or fifteen years earlier, for the philosophers who rushed to Husserl's unpublished archives when his major works were still to a large extent unpublished in French.

I will start with the relationship with American sociology, which, in its most visible expression – what I called the Capitoline triad of Parsons, Merton and Lazarsfeld – subjected social science to a whole series of reductions and impoverishments, from which, it seemed to me, it had to be freed, in particular by a return (encouraged by Lévi-Strauss) to the works of Durkheim and the Durkheimians (especially Mauss) and Max Weber (revitalized by a reading that broke with the neo-Kantian reduction performed by Aron), two immense authors who had been annexed, and watered down, by Parsons. To fight against that new and socially very powerful orthodoxy (Aron himself devoted two years of his seminar to Parsons, and Lazarsfeld taught, for a year, in front of the whole world of French sociology, assembled by Boudon and Lécuyer – not quite the whole of it: there was at least one absence ... – the rudiments of the 'methodology' that the scientific multinational he had built up was laying down worldwide), one needed to resort to realistic strategies and refuse two complementary temptations (with the aid of the sociology of sociology and, in particular, of work such as Michael Pollak's

(1979)): on the one hand, the temptation of pure and simple submission to the dominant definition of social science, and on the other, a retreat into national ignorance, which entailed, for example, an a priori refusal of statistical methods, which were associated with American positivism, a position perhaps most visibly championed by Lucien Goldmann, together with some Marxists who regarded as suspect in principle any reference to Max Weber or the English-language literature, of which they were often largely ignorant (it was to fight this politically encouraged and reinforced 'national' insularity, among other things, that, first with the Éditions de Minuit Sens Commun series and then with the journal *Actes de la recherche en sciences sociales*, I undertook to widen access to major foreign researchers, both classics, like Cassirer, and contemporaries, such as Goffman, Labov, etc.).

In the battle against the theoretical and methodological orthodoxy that dominated the scientific world, I tried to find allies in Germany, but the split between academic theorists (the Frankfurt School, Habermas, then Luhmann) and empiricists submissive to the American orthodoxy was (and remains) too strong, practically unbridgeable. There was in my project, as I explained it to German friends, a political, but specific, intention: it was to create a realistic third way, capable of leading to a new way of doing social science, by taking the weapons of the adversary (statistical ones, in particular – but in France we also had a great tradition of statistical work, with INSEE, the national statistical institute, from which I learned a lot) and turn those weapons against him, by reactivating European traditions that had been distorted and deformed by their transporting to America (Durkheim and the Durkheimians, who were extensively republished in the Sens Commun series; Weber, revived by an active rereading, or more precisely by a free reinterpretation that rescued him from both Parsons and Aron; Schutz and the phenomenology of the social world, etc.). The aim was to escape from the forced choice between the simple importers of second-hand methods and concepts and the Marxists and their associates, who were stuck in their refusal of Weber and empirical sociology. (In this respect, the policy of translating foreign texts was a key element – I am thinking for example of Labov, whose work and active presence were the launch pad for the development of a genuine sociolinguistics in France, reconnecting with the European tradition from which he had originally come.) All this was done with the ambition of finding an international base for this new science, through training activities directed particularly towards Hungary, which was gently breaking free from 'dialectical materialism' and discovering statistics (of poverty, in particular), Algeria, then leading the way in the struggles of the Third World, and Brazil.

But I was no less strongly opposed to philosophy, whether it was the institutional philosophers who clung to the defence of the *agrégation* and its archaic syllabi, and especially the aristocratic philosophy of philosophy as a caste of higher essence, or all the philosophers who, in spite of their anti-institutional mood and, in some cases their flaunted break with 'philosophies of the subject', continued to profess the statutory contempt for the social sciences that was one of the pillars of the traditional philosophical credo – I am thinking of Althusser referring to the '*so-called* social sciences', or Foucault placing the social sciences in the lower order of 'knowledges'. I could not fail to feel a certain irritation at what seemed to me to be a double-game played by these philosophers, who would take over the object of the social sciences, while seeking to undermine their foundation. My resistance to philosophy sprang from no hostility towards that discipline, and it was still in the name of an elevated (perhaps too elevated) conception of philosophy that I tried to contribute to a sociology of philosophy that could contribute greatly to philosophy by ridding it of the doxic philosophy of philosophy which is one of the effects of the constraints and routines of the philosophical institution.

It is no doubt the very singular situation of philosophy in France, resulting in particular from the (quite unique) existence of philosophy teaching in secondary education, and the dominant position of philosophy in academic hierarchies, that explains the particular force of the philosophical subversion that appeared in France in the 1970s (one would need to offer here a model analogous to the one I put forward to explain the exceptional strength of the movement of anti-academic subversion that appeared in France, with Manet and the impressionists, and the contrasting absence of such a movement in Britain, for lack of a similar concentration of symbolic powers in artistic matters).

But the movement of the French philosophers who achieved fame in the 1970s owes its ambiguity to the fact that the revolt against the university institution was combined with a *conservative revolution* against the threat that the rise of the social sciences, especially through 'structuralist' linguistics and anthropology, represented for the hegemony of philosophy (I have analysed the social context of the relationship between philosophy and the social sciences in more detail in *Homo Academicus* and especially in the preface to the English edition (1988a) and the second French edition of 1992). By virtue of the academic trajectory that led them to the apex of the French university institution at a time when that institution was entering a deep crisis, these philosophers were inspired by a particularly strong anti-institutional temperament against a particularly rigid, closed and oppressive institution, and as a consequence they responded in a 'providentially' adjusted way (without, of course, at all seeking to do so) to the expectations aroused by the 'revolution' of 1968, a specific revolution, which brought politico-intellectual contestation into the university field (meanwhile Feyerabend in Berlin and Kuhn in the USA were also being used to provide a language for a spontaneous calling into question of science). But in addition, haunted by the need to maintain their hegemony over the social sciences, they paradoxically adopted the historicist critique of truth (and of the sciences) for their own purposes, while radicalizing it, in a strategy very close to that of Heidegger ontologizing historicism (Bourdieu 1991b).

The 1970s saw a sudden reversal of the dominant philosophical mood. Up to then, philosophy (at least in Britain and America and even on the Continent) had aspired to logic, aiming to construct a unitary formal system based on Russell's analysis of mathematics; analytical philosophy, the logical empiricism of Hempel, Carnap and Reichenbach, great admirers of the early Wittgenstein (the *Tractatus*), and also phenomenology, followed Frege in refusing to make any concessions to 'historicism' and 'psychologism'; all declared the same determination to make a clear distinction between formal or logical questions and empirical questions, which were seen as non-rational or even irrational – in particular, they denounced the 'genetic fallacy' of mixing empirical considerations with logical justifications. This collective conversion, a kind of unbridled revenge of the 'genetic fallacy', 'symbolized', in France, by the transition from Koyré and Vuillemin to Foucault and Deleuze, made the attachment to formal, universal truths appear outmoded and even somewhat reactionary, compared with the analysis of particular historical-cultural situations, illustrated by Foucault's texts, which, brought together under the title *Power/Knowledge*, shaped his American reputation (on the 1970s as a turning-point in the USA, see Toulmin 1977: 143–4). [It would be easy to show that, while remaining rooted in the most aristocratic philosophy of philosophy, this transformation of the philosophical mood was very directly linked, both in its style and in its objects, to the experiences and influence of May '68 which led philosophers and philosophy to discover politics or, as they like to say, 'the political'.]

I think that this analysis, however much it simplifies, enables one to understand – it certainly enables me to understand – why I have constantly found myself out of step with those whom campus radic-

alism has generically placed under the umbrella category of 'postmodernists' (those who are interested in 'reception theory' would probably find in this disjunction the key to the way my work has been
received in the USA: is he modern or postmodern, a sociologist or a
philosopher; or, secondarily, is he an anthropologist or a sociologist;
or even, is he right-wing or left-wing? – Bourdieu 1996). Having left
philosophy for sociology (a 'defection' which, from the standpoint of
those who remain attached to the title of philosopher, makes all the
difference in the world), I was bound, as an aspiring scientist, to
remain committed to the rationalist vision – rather than simply
using the social sciences, like Foucault or Derrida, so as to reduce
them or destroy them, while practising them without saying so and
without paying the price of a genuine conversion to the constraints
and demands of empirical research. Strongly rooted in a 'hard-core'
philosophical tradition (Leibniz, Husserl, Cassirer, the history and
philosophy of the sciences, etc.) and not having gone to sociology
by some negative choice (Georges Canguilhem, with whom I had
registered a thesis topic, which I subsequently repudiated, had
mapped out for me a career as a philosopher modelled on his own,
with a post as a philosophy teacher in Toulouse, combined with
medical studies), I was not inclined to compensatory behaviours of
the type that lead some sociologists or historians, less sure of themselves, to 'play the philosopher'. I made a point – following in this
respect the kind of aristocratism of refusal which in my eyes characterized Canguilhem – of systematically confining to notes or paren-
theses the reflexions that might have been called 'philosophical' (I am
thinking for example of one of the few explicit discussions that I
devoted to Foucault, which is relegated to the final note of an obscure
article in the journal *Études rurales* (1989), in which I returned to the
research I had done thirty years earlier on peasant celibacy.) Always
firmly bearing the title of sociologist, I quite consciously excluded (at
the cost of a loss of symbolic capital that I entirely accepted) the
widespread strategies of the 'double game' and the double profit
(sociologist and philosopher, philosopher and historian) which, I
have to admit, were profoundly antipathetic to me, not least because
they seemed to me to announce a lack of ethical and scientific rigour
(Bourdieu 1996).

   Not surprisingly, then, by virtue of the same logic, I could not enter
into the debates on science as they were conducted in the 1970s. In
fact, having very naturally encountered, as a sociologist, the problem
of the social context of science that others discover only indirectly, I
was content to pursue my craft as a sociologist by subjecting science
and the scientific field, which for me was an object like others (except

that it gave me an opportunity to take on one of the pillars of the Capitoline triad, Robert Merton), to sociological analysis – instead of settling scores with (social) science as did the 'postmodern' philosophers and, in different styles, all the new 'philosopher-sociologists' of science. There is no need to resort to extraordinary means of effecting a break (such as reference, as equivocal as it is ennobling, to Wittgenstein) in order to subject the logicist and scientistic visions to sociological critique; no need, either, for ostentatious breaks with the rationalist tradition to which I was attached by my training (in history and philosophy of science), by my philosophical orientation, and also by my position as a researcher. And I did not cease to look to Bachelard and the French tradition of epistemology, in my effort to found an epistemology of the social sciences on a constructivist philosophy of science (which anticipated Kuhn but without turning purely and simply into the relativism of the postmodernists), as much as in my analysis of the scientific field. The break, which seemed to me a necessary one, with the 'native' view of science, more or less relayed by the scientistic (Mertonian) vision, did not lead either to a questioning or to a legitimation of science (in particular social science), and my position of twofold refusal (neither Merton nor Bloor and Collins, neither nihilist relativism nor scientism) would once again put me out of phase in the debates of the new sociologists of science, which I had helped to launch.

This apparently tepid, prudent position no doubt also owes a lot to the dispositions of a habitus which inclines me towards refusal of the 'heroic', 'revolutionary', 'radical', or rather 'radical chic' posture, in short of postmodern radicalism identified with philosophical profundity – and, in politics, a rejection of 'gauchisme' (unlike Foucault and Deleuze), but also of the Communist Party or Mao (in contrast to Althusser). Likewise it is no doubt the dispositions of the habitus that explain the antipathy inspired in me by phrase-makers and self-publicists and the respect I feel for the 'toilers of proof', to use a Bachelardian phrase, and all those who now, in sociology and the history of science, quietly perpetuate the tradition of the philosophy and history of the sciences inaugurated by Bachelard, Canguilhem, Koyré or Vuillemin.

But perhaps all these refusals had no other basis than the intuition that these ultra-radical poses and postures are simply the inversion of authoritarian and conservative, or cynical and opportunistic positions. This intuition of the habitus has been amply confirmed by the fluctuations of so many subsequent trajectories in response to the forces of the field, with for example the shift from 'everything is political' to 'everything is moral'. The constancy of habitus may manifest itself in the inversion of position-takings when the space of possibles is inverted (I could analyse here, for example, all kinds of superficially unlikely reversals, such as leaps from Heidegger to Wittgenstein, or the Althusserians' misunderstandings over the Vienna Circle and Austrian philosophy, which, for those old enough to remember it, very exactly recalls the treatment of Heidegger by the fashionable Marxists; not to mention, in politics, the 'coat-turning', as some would call it, that has led so many contemporaries from ultra-bolshevism to ultra-liberalism, tempered or not by a highly opportune – and opportunistic – social-liberalism).

Method would require one to examine the present state of the field of sociology and the field of the social sciences with a view to understanding individual and collective trajectories (in particular those of the group that I led) in relation to the changes in the symbolic power relations within each of these two fields and between them (carefully distinguishing the two kinds of scientific capital-power). It can at least be said that the position of sociology in the space of the disciplines has changed enormously, as has the structure of the sociological field – and that is no doubt what gives me the possibility of saying what I now say, and could not have said thirty years ago, in particular the project of transforming the field, which, at that time, would have seemed senseless or, more precisely, megalomaniac and reducible to the particularities of one person (something of that persists when people characterize the research group that I built up, the Centre de sociologie européenne, as a *sect*, failing to understand and accept the overarching intention of a collective, cumulative scientific project, which would integrate the theoretical and technical advances of the discipline, in a logic akin to that of the natural sciences, and be based on a common set of explicit philosophical choices, in particular as regards the anthropological presuppositions implied in all 'human sciences').

One would also need to consider my own trajectory within this field, taking into account – to avoid the somewhat simplistic use often made of the notion of the 'mandarin' (itself rather simplistic and sociologically inadequate) – the specific character of the position of the Collège de France, the least institutional (or the most anti-institutional) of French academic institutions and, as I showed in *Homo Academicus* (1988a), the home of the consecrated heretics. One would need to examine the scope and significance of the 'revolution' that was brought about, which, while it succeeded at the symbolic level (at least abroad), fairly indisputably failed in terms of the French academic institution, as can be seen from the subsequent fate of the group, whose members ended up relegated to secondary, marginal or minor positions within the French university system. The difficulty encountered in the attempt to found a 'school' (of thought) is similar to that which Émile Durkheim experienced in his own time (although he understood better than anyone that you cannot become a 'school of thought' without gaining a foothold in the school, and battled to do so). One would need to analyse the function of the journal *Actes de la recherche en sciences sociales* as an instrument of reproduction independent of academic reproduction, which is largely controlled by the holders of temporal powers, with the latter tending, as I have said, to be 'national'. Finally, one would need to analyse the cost of prolonged membership of the group, responsibility for which is attributed to the founder and the other leaders of the group, although it is to a large extent the effect of the social mechanisms of rejection (perhaps this is another case of 'reproduction forbidden' . . .).

I have already hinted at the analysis of the habitus by mentioning several times the role of socially constituted dispositions in my position-takings and, in particular, in my sympathies or antipathies for various ideas or persons. I am no exception to the social law that geographical and social position play a decisive part in practices, in relationship with the social spaces within which the dispositions that it favours are realized.

One's social past is particularly burdensome when it comes to doing social science – whatever that past and that identity may be, working-class or bourgeois, male or female. Always intertwined with the past that psychoanalysis explores, and translated or converted into a scholastic past to which the verdicts of the educational system sometimes give the force of a destiny, it continues to exert its pressure throughout a whole existence. It is well known, for example, albeit somewhat abstractly, that differences in social origin continue to orient practices throughout a whole lifetime and to determine the social success that is granted to them. But it was not without some surprise that I was able to verify that *normaliens* from different social origins, although apparently 'equalized' by passing the same competitive examination and possessing a qualification that is socially homogenizing (by virtue of the very distinction it asserts relative to all others), went on to have profoundly different careers, especially in academic terms, that were to some degree proportionate to their initial status (Bourdieu 1975b).

I shall not dwell here – it would be too difficult in the context of a public lecture – on the properties of the family into which I was born. My father was the son of a peasant sharecropper, but when he was about thirty, that is to say, roughly at the time I was born, he became a junior state employee and worked for the rest of his life as a clerk in a particularly remote village in Béarn (although it was less than 20 kilometres from Pau, my classmates at the lycée had never heard of it, and joked about it). I think that my childhood experience as the son of someone who had 'crossed over' to the other side (which I recognized in Sartre's sketch of Paul Nizan in his introduction to *Aden Arabie*) probably weighed heavily in the formation of my dispositions towards the social world: I felt very close to my primary-school classmates, the children of smallholders, artisans or shopkeepers, with whom I had almost everything in common, except the academic success that somewhat marked me out, but I was separated from them by a kind of invisible barrier, which was sometimes expressed in ritual insults directed at *lous emplegats*, white-collar workers, 'always in the shade', rather as my father was separated (and he showed many signs of suffering on account of it, such as the fact that he always voted far-left) from these peasants (and from his father and brother who had stayed on the farm and whom he went to help every year when he took his annual leave), to whom he was all the same very close (especially in the devoted services he rendered them, with infinite patience), some at least of whom were considerably better off than him. (You must find the language I use very confused, but – and this is another of those indelible differences – not all life 'stories' are equally easy and agreeable to tell, not least because social origin, especially for someone like me, who has shown the importance of this variable, is predisposed to play the role of an instrument and a stake in struggles and polemics, and to be used in the most different ways, but almost always for the worse ...)

One would also need to analyse the no doubt deeply 'structuring' experience of boarding school, especially through the discovery of a social difference, inverted this time, from the 'bourgeois' city-dwellers, and the separation between the world of the boarding school (Flaubert writes somewhere that someone who has known it, at the age of ten, knows almost everything about life), a terrifying apprenticeship in social realism, where everything is already present – opportunism, self-interested servility, betrayal, treachery, denunciation, etc. – and the world of the classroom, where entirely opposite values predominated, and the teachers, especially the women, who offered a world of intellectual discoveries and human relationships that could be called 'enchanted'. I came to understand recently that my very profound investment in the academic institution was probably constituted in this dual experience, and that the deep sense of revolt, which has never left me, against the educational system as it still is, no doubt stems from the immense, inconsolable disappointment produced in me by the discrepancy between the hateful, nocturnal face of the school system and its supremely respectable, diurnal face (and the same thing could be said, *mutatis mutandis*, of my relation to intellectuals).

To avoid overburdening the analysis *ad infinitum*, I would like to move rapidly to what seems to me now, in the present state of my effort at reflexivity, to be the essential point: the fact that the contradictory coincidence of election into the educational aristocracy with lower-class and provincial (I would like to say: *very* provincial) origins underlay the constitution of a *cleft habitus*, generating all kinds of contradictions and tensions. It is not easy to describe the effects, that is to say the dispositions, engendered by this kind of *coincidentia oppositorum*. On the one hand, a recalcitrant disposition, especially towards the educational system, an alma mater with two contrasting faces which, no doubt because it was given the excessive attachment of an oblate, was also the object of a violent, constant revolt springing from debt and disappointment. On the other hand, the self-assurance, even arrogance of the 'hyper-selected' student, who comes to see himself as the product of a miracle, yet self-created, capable of rising to every challenge (I see a paradigmatic example of this in the mean trick that Heidegger plays on the Kantians when he robs them of one of the pillars of rationalism by discovering the finitude at the heart of the transcendental Aesthetic). The ambivalence towards the university world and the intellectual world that resulted from this condemned my whole relationship to those worlds to appear as incomprehensible or misplaced, whether it was exalted, reformist indignation or a spontaneous distance from academic consecrations (I remember one commentator who remarked indignantly on the critical reflexivity of my inaugural lecture, without seeing that this was the necessary condition for making the experience bearable) or a lucidity about academic ways and humours that cannot be expressed, either in everyday remarks or in books (Bourdieu 1988a, 1988b), without being seen as the treason of one who 'bites the hand that feeds him', or, worse, 'lets the cat out of the bag'.

This ambivalence is the source of a *double distance* with respect to the opposing positions, dominant and dominated, within the field. I am thinking for example of my attitude in politics, which distances me both from aristocratism and from populism, and of the recalcitrant posture which, outside of any imperative of civic or moral virtue, but also without any calculation, almost always orients me against the tide, leading me to declare myself ostentatiously Weberian or Durkheimian at a time, around 1968, when it was fashionable to be Marxist, or, by contrast, as nowadays, to enter into a kind of fairly solitary dissidence when everyone seems to find it more opportune to rally to the social (and 'socialist') order. No doubt this happens in part as a reaction against the positions taken by those who follow the inclinations of habitus different from my own and whose opportunistic conformism is particularly antipathetic to me when it takes the form of a politically correct espousal of good causes. I cannot resist here quoting Jacques Bouveresse (with whom my habitus often leads me to identify): 'Musil says of his hero Ulrich, in *A Man without Qualities*, that he loved mathematics because of all the people who could not stand it. I initially loved mathematical logic partly for similar reasons, because of the contempt and fear it generally aroused in the philosophers around me' (Bouveresse 2001: 198).

But it is no doubt in the particular style of my research, in the type of objects that interest me and my way of approaching them that one would find the clearest manifestation of a cleft scientific habitus, the product of a 'conciliation of contraries' which perhaps inclines me to 'reconcile contraries'. I am thinking of the way I have invested great theoretical ambitions in often very trivial empirical objects, tackling the question of the temporal structures of consciousness through the relation to the future of sub-proletarians, the ritual questions of (especially Kantian) aesthetics through everyday photography, the question of fetishism through *haute couture* and the price of perfumes, the problem of social classes on the occasion of a problem of coding, all evidence of a simultaneously ambitious and 'modest' way of doing science. Perhaps what are called 'humble' origins give in this case virtues that are not taught in manuals of methodology, such as the lack of any disdain for patient, painstaking empirical work; a taste for humble objects (I think of artists who, like Patrick Saytour, rehabilitate despised, 'common' materials, such as linoleum); an indifference to disciplinary boundaries and the social hierarchy of domains, which has disposed me to combine the highest and the lowest, the hottest and the coldest; the anti-intellectualist disposition which, intellectually cultivated, underlies the theory of practice engaged in scientific work (for example, in the role given to intuition), and which leads to an anti-scholastic use of concepts excluding both theoreticist exhibitionism and the false rigour of positivism (which has resulted in some misunderstandings with methodologists separated from practice, including one or two who write about the notion of habitus); the sense of and taste for the tacit knowledge and know-how that are invested for example in the devising of a questionnaire or a coding schedule. And it must have been the antagonistic dispositions of a cleft habitus that encouraged me to make, and enabled me to succeed in, the dangerous move from a sovereign discipline, philosophy, to a stigmatized discipline like sociology, while importing into the 'lower' discipline the high ambitions associated with the original discipline and the scientific virtues capable of fulfilling them (Ben-David and Collins 1966).

Contrary to what the imperative of *Wertfreiheit* demands, experience linked to one's social past can and must be mobilized in research, on condition that it has previously been submitted to a rigorous critical examination. The relation to the past which remains present and active in the form of the habitus has to be socioanalysed. Through the liberating anamnesis that it fosters, socioanalysis makes it possible to rationalize scientific strategies, without cynicism. It allows one to understand the game instead of undergoing it or suffering from it, and even, up to a point, to 'learn lessons' from it – for example, by taking advantage of the revelations which may be brought to each of us by the self-interested lucidity of competitors or by bringing to consciousness the social foundations of intellectual affinities.

Thus the sociology of education may play a decisive role in what Bachelard called the 'psychoanalysis of the scientific mind', and I have no doubt enormously benefited in my work, and not only in the area of education, from the quite particular lucidity of someone who has remained marginal while reaching the most central sites of the system. But this lucidity has constantly fed on itself, in and through a constant effort to ask of sociology the means of exploring more profoundly the social unconscious of the sociologist (I am thinking for example of the analysis of the categories of professorial understanding – Bourdieu, 1975b).

One of the foundations of this dimension of scientific competence, commonly called 'intuition' or 'creative imagination', is no doubt to be found in the scientific use of a social experience previously subjected to sociological critique. I would need to relate here in detail (but I have done so recently, in a lecture entitled 'Participant objectivation' – Bourdieu 2002) the kind of experimentation on the work of reflexivity that I did at the time of the fieldwork which led to the article 'Célibat et condition paysanne' (1962): having become aware that I was using my primary social experience to defend myself against the spontaneous sociology of my Kabyle informants, I wanted to go back to the source of that experience and take it as my object; I discovered, in connection with two examples – on the one hand the notion of *besiat*, the neighbourhood, the set of neighbours, which some ethnologists had constituted as a social unit, and on the other hand apropos of an informant's remark about the reasons one can have for 'cousining up' ('they've become very "kith and kin" now that there's a *Polytechnicien* in the family') – that the genealogical model and the ideas generally accepted regarding kinship prevent one from grasping the true nature of the reproduction strategies through which groups are maintained and indeed the very mode of existence of these groups. In short, it is clear that any social experience, perhaps especially when accompanied by crises, conversions and reconversions, can be converted from a handicap into capital, so long as it is mastered through analysis.

I have constantly repeated that the sociology of sociology is not a division of sociology among others; that one needs to draw on the gains of sociological science in order to do sociology; that the sociology of sociology should always accompany the practice of sociology. But, while there is value in self-awareness, sociological vigilance is not enough. Reflexivity takes on its full efficacy only when it is embodied in collectives which have so much incorporated it that they practise it as a reflex. In a research group of that kind, the collective censorship is very strong, but it is a liberating censorship, which leads one to dream of the censorship of an ideally constituted field that would free each of the participants from the 'biases' linked to his or her position and dispositions.

Conclusion

I know that I am caught up and comprehended in the world that I take as my object. I cannot take up a position, as a scientist, on the struggles over the truth of the social world without knowing that I am doing so, that the only truth is that truth is a stake in struggles as much within the scientific world (the sociological field) as in the social world that this scientific world takes as its object (every agent has his 'idiotic' vision of the world, which he aims to impose – insult, for example, being a form of wild exercise of symbolic power) and with respect to which its struggles over truth are engaged. In saying that, and in recommending the practice of reflexivity, I am also aware of handing over to others instruments which they can turn against me to subject me to objectivation – but in so doing, they show that I am right.

Because the truth of the social world is the object of struggles in the social world and in the sociological world which is committed to producing the truth of the social world, the struggle for the truth of the social world is necessarily endless. (And social science will never come to the end of the effort to impose itself as a science.) Truth is the generalized relativity of points of view, apart from the one which constitutes them as such by constituting the space of points of view. I cannot avoid thinking of a metaphor that I have already used: borrowed from Leibniz, it consists in regarding God as the 'geometral of all perspectives', the locus where all partial points of view are integrated and reconciled, the absolute point of view from which the world presents itself as a spectacle, a unified and unitary spectacle, the view without a point of view, the 'view from nowhere and from everywhere' of a God without place who is at once everywhere and nowhere. But this 'geometral of all perspectives' is nothing other than the field in which, as I have constantly said, the antagonistic points of view clash in accordance with regulated procedures and are gradually integrated, through rational confrontation. This is a gain which the individual sociologist, however great the contribution he may make to the structure and functioning of the field, must take care not to forget – just as he must not forget that, if, like any other scientist, he tries to contribute to the construction of the point of view without a point of view which is the point of view of the scientist, as a social agent he is caught up in the object that he takes as his object, and that in this capacity he has a point of view which does not coincide either with that of others or with the bird's eye view of the quasi-divine spectator which he can attain if he fulfils the demands of the field. He knows therefore that the particularity of the social sciences requires him to work (as I tried to show for the cases of the gift and work in *Pascalian Meditations* (1999a)) towards constructing a scientific truth capable of integrating the observer's vision and the truth of the practical vision of the agent as a point of view which is unaware of being a point of view and is experienced in the illusion of absoluteness.

Bibliography

Abragam, A. 1989: *Time Reversal: An Autobiography*. Oxford: Clarendon.

Aron, R. 1962: *Paix et Guerre entre les nations*. Paris: Calmann-Lévy.

Barnes, B. 1974: *Scientific Knowledge and Sociological Theory*. London: Routledge & Kegan Paul.

Barnes, B. and Bloor, D. 1982: 'Relativism, rationalism and sociology of knowledge'. In M. Hollis and S. Lukes (eds), *Rationality and Relativism*, Oxford: Blackwell.

Ben-David, J. 1991: *Scientific Growth: Essays on the Social Organization and Ethos of Science*. Berkeley: University of California Press.

Ben-David, J. and Collins, R. 1966: 'Social factors in the origins of a new science: the case of psychology', *American Sociological Review*, 31: 451–65 (repr. in Ben-David 1991: 49–70).

Biagioli, M. 1998: 'The instability of authorship: credit and responsibility in contemporary biomedecine', *FASEB Journal*, 12: 3–16.

Bitbol, M. 1996: *Mécanique quantique, une introduction philosophique*. Paris: Flammarion.

Bloor, D. 1983: *Wittgenstein: A Social Theory of Knowledge*. New York: Columbia University Press.

Bloor, D. 1991: *Knowledge and Social Imagery* (2nd edn). Chicago: University of Chicago Press.

Bloor, D. 1992: 'Left and right Wittgensteinians'. In Pickering 1992.

Bourdieu, P. 1962: 'Célibat et condition paysanne', *Études rurales*, 5–6: 32–136.

Bourdieu, P. 1975a: 'La spécificité du champ scientifique et les conditions sociales du progrès de la raison', *Sociologie et Sociétés*, 7(1): 91–118. Translations: 'The specificity of the scientific field and the social conditions of the progress of reason', *Social Science Information* (Paris), 14(6) (1975): 19–47; also in C. C. Lemert (ed.), *French Sociology*, New York: Columbia University Press, 1981, 257–92; and in M. Biagioli (ed.), *The Science Studies Reader*, London: Routledge, 1999. See also 'Le champ scientifique', *Actes de la recherche en sciences sociales*, 2–3 (1976): 88–104.

Bourdieu, P. (with M. de Saint Martin) 1975b: 'Les catégories de l'entendement professoral', *Actes de la recherche en sciences sociales*, 3: 68–93.

Bourdieu, P. 1984: *Distinction: A Social Critique of the Judgement of Taste*. Cambridge, Mass.: Harvard University Press.

Bourdieu, P. 1988a: *Homo Academicus*. Cambridge: Polity; Stanford, Calif.: Stanford University Press.

Bourdieu, P. 1988b: 'Préface'. In B. Mazon, *Aux origines de l'École des hautes études en sciences sociales. Le rôle du mécénat américain*, Paris: Éditions du Cerf, i–v.

Bourdieu, P. 1989: 'Reproduction interdite: la dimension symbolique de la domination économique', *Études rurales*, 113–14: 15–36.

Bourdieu, P. 1990: 'Animadversiones in Mertonem'. In J. Clark, C. Modgil and S. Modgil (eds), *Robert K. Merton: Consensus and Controversy*, London: Falmer Press, 297–301.

Bourdieu, P. 1991a: *Language and Symbolic Power*. Cambridge, Mass.: Harvard University Press.

Bourdieu, P. 1991b: *The Political Ontology of Martin Heidegger*. Stanford: Stanford University Press.

Bourdieu, P. 1995: 'Sur les rapports entre la sociologie et l'histoire en Allemagne et en France' (discussion with L. Raphael), *Actes de la recherche en sciences sociales*, 106–7: 108–22.

Bourdieu, P. 1996: 'Passport to Duke'. In M. Sabour, 'Pierre Bourdieu's thought in contemporary social sciences', *International Journal of Contemporary Sociology*, 33(2): 145–50.

Bourdieu, P. 1999a: *Pascalian Meditations*. Cambridge: Polity; Stanford: Stanford University Press.

Bourdieu, P. 1999b: 'Une révolution conservatrice dans l'édition', *Actes de la recherche en sciences sociales*, 126–7: 3–28.

Bourdieu, P. 2001a: *Contre-feux 2. Pour un mouvement social européen*. Paris: Raisons d'agir.

Bourdieu, P. 2001b: *Langage et pouvoir symbolique* rev. and enlarged edn. Paris: Éditions du Seuil.

Bourdieu, P. 2002: 'Participant objectivation. Breaching the boundary between anthropology and sociology: How?', lecture on the occasion of the presentation of the Huxley Memorial Medal for 2000, Royal Anthropological Institute, London, 6 Dec. 2000.

Bourdieu, P. and Passeron, J.-C. 1967: 'Sociology and philosophy in France since 1945: death and resurrection of a philosophy without subject', *Social Research*, 34(1): 162–212.

Bourdieu, P., Boltanski, L., Castel, R. and Chamboredon, J.-C. 1990: *Photography: A Middle-Brow Art*. Cambridge: Polity; Stanford: University

Press. (First French edition 1965: *Un Art moyen, essai sur les usages sociaux de la photographie*, Paris: Éditions de Minuit; revised edn 1970.)

Bourdieu, P., Chamboredon J.-C. and Passeron J.-C. 1991: *The Craft of Sociology: Epistemological Preliminaries*. New York and Berlin: De Gruyter. (First French edition 1968: *Le Métier de sociologue*, Paris: Mouton-Bordas.)

Bourdieu, P., Darbel, A., Rivet, J.-P. and Seibel, C. 1963: *Travail et Travailleurs en Algérie*. Paris and The Hague: Mouton.

Bouveresse, J. 1999: *Prodiges et vertiges de l'analogie*. Paris: Raisons d'agir.

Bouveresse, J. 2001: *Essais. L'Époque, la mode, la morale, la satire*, II. Marseille: Agone.

Callon, M. 1986: 'Some elements of a sociology of translation: domestication of the scallops and the fishermen of St-Brieux Bay'. In J. Law (ed.), *Power, Action and Belief: A New Sociology of Knowledge*, London, Routledge & Kegan Paul, 196–233.

Carnap, R. 1950: 'Empiricism, semantics and ontology', *Revue internationale de philosophie*, 4: 20–40 (repr. in the supplement to Carnap, *Meaning and Necessity: A Study in Semantics and Modal Logic*, enlarged edn, Chicago: University of Chicago Press, 1956).

Cole, S. and Cole, J. R. 1967: 'Scientific output and recognition: a study in the operation of the reward system in science', *American Sociological Review*, 32(3): 377–90.

Cole, S. and Zuckerman, H. 1975: 'The emergence of a scientific speciality: the self-exemplifying case of the sociology of science'. In L. A. Coser (ed.) *The Idea of Social Structure: Papers in Honor of Robert K. Merton*, New York: Harcourt Brace Jovanovich, 139–74.

Collins, H. M. (ed.) 1981: *Knowledge and Controversy: Studies in Modern Natural Science*, special issue of *Social Studies of Science*, 11(1).

Collins, H. M. 1985: *Changing Order*. London: Sage.

Collins, H. M. and Yearley, S. 1992: 'Epistemological chicken'. In Pickering 1992: 301–26.

Fleck, L. 1979: *Genesis and Development of a Scientific Fact*. Chicago: University of Chicago Press.

Frege, G. 1953: *The Foundations of Arithmetic: A Logico-Mathematical Enquiry into the Concept of Number* (2nd, rev. edn). Oxford: Blackwell.

Friedman, M. 1996: 'Overcoming metaphysics: Carnap and Heidegger'. In R. N. Giere and A. W. Richardson (eds), *Origins of Logical Empiricism*, Minneapolis: Minnesota University Press.

Friedman, M. 1998: 'On the sociology of scientific knowledge and its philosophical agenda', *Studies in History and Philosophy of Science*, 29(2): 239–71.

Garfield, E. 1975: 'The obliteration phenomenon', *Current Contents*, 51–2: 5–7.

Garfinkel, H. and Sachs, H. 1986: 'On formal structures of practical action'. In H. Garfinkel (ed.), *Ethnomethodological Studies of Work*, London, Routledge & Kegan Paul, 160–93.

Geison, G. L. 1995: *The Private Science of Louis Pasteur*. Princeton: Princeton University Press.

Gilbert, G. N. and Mulkay, M. 1984: *Opening Pandora's Box: A Sociological Analysis of Scientists' Discourse*. Cambridge: Cambridge University Press.

Gingras, Y. 1991: *Physics and the Rise of Scientific Research in Canada*. Montreal: McGill-Queen's University Press.

Gingras, Y. 1995: 'Un air de radicalisme: sur quelques tendances récentes de la sociologie de la science et de la technologie', *Actes de la recherche en sciences sociales*, 108: 3–17.

Gingras, Y. 2000: 'Pourquoi le "programme fort" est-il incompris?', *Cahiers internationaux de sociologie*, 109: 235–55.

Gingras, Y. 2001: 'What did mathematics do to physics', *Cahiers d'épistémologie* (University of Quebec), 274; also in *History of Science* (Dec. 2001).

Gingras, Y. 2002: 'Mathématisation et exclusion, socioanalyse de la formation des cités savantes'. In J. J. Wunenburger (ed.), *Gaston Bachelard et l'épistémologie française*, Paris: PUF.

Grmek, M. D. 1973: *Raisonnement experimental et recherches toxicologiques chez Claude Bernard*. Geneva: Droz.

Grünbaum, A. 1984: *The Foundations of Psychoanalysis: A Philosophical Critique*. Berkeley: University of California Press.

Hacking, I. 1992: 'The self-vindication of laboratory sciences'. In Pickering 1992: 29–64.

Hagstrom, W. O. 1965: *The Scientific Community*. New York: Basic Books.

Hannaway, O. 1988: 'Laboratory design and the aim of science', *Isis*, 77: 585–610.

Hargens, L. 1978: 'Theory and method in the sociology of science'. In J. Gaston (ed.), *Sociology of Science*, San Francisco: Jossey-Bass, 121–39.

Haskell, T. L. 1984: 'Professionalism versus capitalism: R. H. Tawney, É. Durkheim and C. S. Peirce on the disinterestedness of professional communities'. In T. L. Haskell (ed.), *The Authority of Experts: Studies in History and Theory*, Bloomington: Indiana University Press.

Heilbron, J. L. and Seidel, R. W. 1989: *Lawrence and his Laboratory: A History of the Lawrence Berkeley Laboratory*. Berkeley: University of California Press.

Holmes, F. L. 1974: *Claude Bernard and Animal Chemistry: The Emergence of a Scientist*. Cambridge, Mass.: Harvard University Press.

Holton, G. H. 1978: 'Presuppositions and the Millikan–Ehrenhaft Dispute'. In G. H. Holton, *The Scientific Imagination: Case Studies*, Cambridge: Cambridge University Press, 25–83.

Knorr-Cetina, K. 1983: 'The ethnographic study of scientific work: towards a constructivist interpretation of science'. In K. Knorr-Cetina and M. Mulkay (eds), *Science Observed: Perspectives in the Social Study of Science*, London: Sage, 115–40.

Knorr-Cetina, K. 1992: 'The couch, the cathedral and the laboratory: on the relationship between experiment and laboratory in science'. In Pickering 1992: 113–38.

Kuhn, T. S. 1962: *The Structure of Scientific Revolutions*. Chicago: University of Chicago Press.

Kuhn, T. S. 1977: *The Essential Tension: Selected Studies in Scientific Tradition and Change*. Chicago: University of Chicago Press.

Laszlo, P. 2000: *Miroir de la chimie*. Paris: Éditions du Seuil.

Latour, B. 1983: 'Le dernier des capitalistes sauvages: interview d'un biochimiste', *Fundamenta Scientiae*, 314 (4): 301–27.

Latour, B. 1987: *Science in Action: How to Follow Scientists and Engineers through Society*. Milton Keynes: Open University Press.

Latour, B. 1988: *The Pasteurization of France*. Cambridge, Mass.: Harvard University Press.

Latour, B. 1993: 'Where are the missing masses? Sociology of a few mundane artefacts'. In W. Bijker and J. Law (eds), *Constructing Networks and Systems*, Cambridge, Mass.: MIT Press.

Latour, B. and Johnson, J. 1988: 'Mixing humans with non-humans: sociology of a door-opener', *Social Problems*, 35: 298–310.

Latour, B. and Woolgar, S. 1979: *Laboratory Life: The Social Construction of Scientific Facts*. London: Sage.

Leontief, W. 1982: 'Academic economics', *Science*, 217: 106–7.

Lynch, M. 1982: 'Art and artifact in laboratory science: a study of shop work and shop talk in a research laboratory', Ph.D diss. University of California, Irvine (see also *Art and Artifact in Laboratory Science*, London: Routledge & Kegan Paul, 1985).

Lynch, M. 1992: 'Extending Wittgenstein: the pivotal move from epistemology to the sociology of science'. In Pickering 1992: 215–65.

Lynch, M. 1993: *Scientific Practice and Ordinary Action: Ethnomethodology and Social Studies of Science*. Cambridge: Cambridge University Press.

Mannheim, K. 1936: *Ideology and Utopia*. London: Kegan Paul.

Marcus, G. E. and Fischer, M. M. J. 1986: *Anthropology as Cultural Critique: An Experimental Moment in the Human Sciences*. Chicago: University of Chicago Press.

Medawar, P. B. 1964: 'Is the scientific paper fraudulent?', *Saturday Review*, 1 Aug. 42–3.

Merleau-Ponty, J. 1965: *Cosmologie du XXe siècle. Étude épistémologique et historique des théories de la cosmologie contemporaine*. Paris: Gallimard.

Merton, R. K. 1957a: 'Bureaucratic structure and personality'. In Merton, *Social Theory and Social Structure*, Glencoe: Free Press, 249–61.

Merton, R. K. 1957b: 'Priorities in scientific discovery: a chapter in the sociology of science', *American Sociological Review*, 22(5): 635–59.

Merton, R. K. 1973: 'The ambivalence of scientists'. In *The Sociology of Science: Theorical and Empirical Investigations*, Chicago: University of Chicago Press, 383–418.

122   *Bibliography*

Mullins, N. C. 1972: 'The development of a scientific speciality: the Phage Group and the origins of molecular biology', *Minerva*, 10(1): 51–82.

Nye, M. J. 1993: *From Chemical Philosophy to Theoretical Chemistry: Dynamics of Matter and Dynamics of Disciplines, 1800–1950*. Berkeley: University of California Press.

Passeron, J.-C. forthcoming: *Le Raisonnement sociologique. Un espace non poppérien de l'argumentation* (2nd rev. edn). Paris: Albin Michel.

Pickering, A. (ed.) 1992: *Science as Practice and Culture*. Chicago: University of Chicago Press.

Poincaré, H. 1968: *La Science et l'Hypothèse*. Paris: Flammarion.

Polanyi, M. 1951: *The Logic of Liberty: Reflections and Rejoinders*. London: Routledge & Kegan Paul.

Pollak, M. 1979: 'Paul F. Lazarsfeld, fondateur d'une multinationale scientifique', *Actes de la recherche en sciences sociales*, 25: 45–59.

Popper, K. R. 1945: *The Open Society and its Enemies*. London: Routledge & Kegan Paul.

Shapin, S. 1988: 'The house of experiment in seventeenth-century England', *Isis*, 79(298): 373–404.

Shapin, S. and Schaffer, S. 1985: *Leviathan and the Air-Pump*. Princeton: Princeton University Press.

Shinn, T. 1988: 'Hiérarchie des chercheurs et formes des recherches', *Actes de la recherche en sciences sociales*, 74: 2–22.

Shinn, T. 2000: 'Formes de division du travail social et convergence intellectuelle: la recherche technico-instrumentale', *Revue française de sociologie*, 3(3): 447–73.

Soulié, C. 1995: 'Anatomie du goût philosophique', *Actes de la recherche en sciences sociales*, 109: 3–28.

Tompkins, J. 1988: 'Fighting words: unlearning to write the critical essay', *Georgia Review*, 43(3): 585–90.

Toulmin, S. 1977: 'From form to function: philosophy and history of science in the 1950s and now', *Daedalus*, 106(3): 143–62.

Wittgenstein, L. 1953: *Philosophical Investigations*. Oxford: Blackwell.

Woolgar, S. (ed.) 1988a: *Knowledge and Reflexivity: New Frontiers in the Sociology of Knowledge*. London: Sage.

Woolgar, S. 1988b: *Science: The Very Idea*. Chichester: Ellis Horwood; London: Tavistock.

Zuckerman, H. A. 1968: 'Patterns of name-ordering among authors of scientific papers: a study of social symbolism and its ambiguity', *American Journal of Sociology*, 74: 276–91.

Index

Lightning Source UK Ltd.
Milton Keynes UK
15 September 2010

159916UK00002B/30/P

9 780745 630601